DISCOVER ATTACHMENT THEORY

showing how our earliest Attachments affect us all throughout our lives

Joan Woodward

First published in 2019 by
Free Association Books

A CIP Catalogue of this book is available from
the British Library

ISBN: 978-1-91138-321-5

Typeset by
Typo•glyphix
www.typoglyphix.co.uk

Cover design by
Candescent

Printed and bound in England

CONTENTS

THE PURPOSE OF THIS BOOK

In 'Understanding Ourselves', Woodward J. 1988 Macmillan, I coined the phrase 'Neurotic Solutions' as a way of describing how we all develop our highly individual sense of ourselves, as a result of how we respond to our 'Attachment' experiences, from birth onwards.

Since then, I have become particularly interested in those people who have deeply rooted patterns of thinking, feeling and behaving, which come from their 'sense of self', which cause them severe suffering; yet they find these patterns equally painful and difficult to 'let go' or change.

I have based this short book on the format of 'The Work in Progress' papers started by Dr. Jean Baker Miller in Welles College, Boston, USA. They consisted of a series of lectures given by different members of The Institute of Relational/Cultural Theory, in a very open and informal way and the papers all included responses from the audience.

I have written it as a 'work in progress' too. Its style is professional, but purposefully NOT academic. This is why I have avoided any full references or indexing. I do refer to other writings, but today all these can so easily be found through the Internet by anyone interested to take them up further. I hope as a result that it can be read easily by anyone interested in Attachment Theory, either because of their work setting, or for themselves. I hope too that the responses to it by a variety of people adds further interest and will lead to others writing more.

I have wanted to update and further clarify my thoughts on 'Neurotic Solutions', as, in the intervening twenty-nine years of continuing working, I have learned a great deal more about the way 'Neurotic Solutions' operate. If this booklet enables any readers to understand and think about this process and then apply it to the ways they relate to themselves or others, it will have served its intended purpose.

DISCOVER ATTACHMENT THEORY

showing how our earliest Attachments affect us all throughout our lives

SECTION ONE

INTRODUCING ATTACHMENT THEORY

Every one of us as human beings needs to have a basic sense of a 'good enough self'. We need to feel we are someone who has been sufficiently wanted, loved and valued to be secure enough to venture out and survive well in this ever increasingly complicated world. This sense of a 'valued self' is the basis of good mental health. What matters is how this sense of 'good enough self' is developed and what happens when it fails to do so.

In the 1970s Dr. John Bowlby defined a new way of understanding human development, which he named 'Attachment Theory'. His work as a psychiatrist and later psychoanalyst was underpinned by his early studies in ecology. This is the name given to the ways all forms of life interact with their environment. This, of course, includes humans. Dr. Bowlby chose to study in great depth the mother/child relationship, as it is a universal one that includes other animals as well as humans.

He turned to the work of other researchers who had made in-depth studies of the way many animals need to stay very close to their mothers from their birth, for safety and their ability to survive. This led Bowlby to recognise that these very early 'Attachments', providing the best prospects for safety and survival, displayed by some animal studies also applied to humans. This led him to study in great detail how all of us as humans are equally dependent on our 'earliest environment' too. This is provided by our 'care givers', as he came to name them. After years of working on the mother/child relationship he recognised that it is **the quality of this relationship from birth onwards that largely determines the state of our mental health for the rest of our lives.**

CHARACTERISTICS OF A 'SECURE ATTACHMENT'

Dr. Bowlby defined the source of our early 'Attachment' experiences as being provided usually in the first instance by our mothers. Nowadays, this more often includes fathers and grandparents too. He describes clearly the ways our 'care givers' need to respond to us in order to provide us with a 'secure Attachment'. These are**: *being physically present*** (this applies most importantly in the early phase of our lives); ***being emotionally responsive to our needs***; relating to us in ways that **feel mutually enjoyable** and also in ways that are **appropriate to our stages of growth.** Some parents find it easy to respond to their children when they are babies, but find their increasing independence and particularly their adolescence is hard to cope with. For other parents, the opposite may be the case.

He recognised two other important characteristics of an 'Attachment'. The first is that it has a **hierarchical aspect** in so far as we all know, even from a very young age, who is our primary Attachment Figure. After that, most of us can probably name four or five people in our lives who matter to us, and then we do not differentiate much at all. He defined the second characteristic as the ability **to endure.** They may change as we get older, for example when our original 'Attachment Figures' have gone our children or friends may take their place. Whether our 'care givers' are able to make us feel 'securely attached', will largely depend on their own early Attachment experiences.

Bowlby and his colleagues worked over many years building up scientific evidence of our human need for 'Secure Attachment', which provides us with our sense of well-being. Although he primarily concentrated on those needs in babies and young people, he also gave recognition to this need lasting, in different forms, throughout our lives. He and his colleagues created tests that can be used with young children and parents, which support these claims. This is not the place to go into great detail about the tests for both children and adults, as these can be found elsewhere, but they have produced consistent results from which reliable conclusions can be drawn.

The tests for small children are done through observations of their behaviour with their mothers: both when they go out of the room, and on their return. For adults, the tests are quite complicated. As someone once remarked, 'a bit like an early therapy session'. What is relevant here is the fact that, when asked about their childhood, many people will say it was 'happy' or 'fine', but when asked to recall what happened when they were ill, or when the family were together at meal times, or weekends, or perhaps on holiday, some of them were able to recognise that things were very different from what they had been describing. They realised how they had pushed such memories out of their immediate awareness. This kind of recognition, when people are able to face it, can sometimes help them to see how their childhood experiences may be affecting their own parenting. From this work came an understanding of the major categories of responses when 'Secure Attachments' fail.

'INSECURE ATTACHMENTS'

These occur when 'care givers' are unable to be sufficiently emotionally responsive to their children's needs and do not experience the relationship with their child with any enjoyment. This is not necessarily the 'care giver's' fault. It can, however, have devastating effects on their children. A mother on her own may be overwhelmed by the demands of a baby. This may be particularly so if she has no or little support and has to earn an income to maintain them both. She may suffer from depression to such a degree that caring for a baby feels quite impossible. She may be feeling excessively anxious or physically ill. The most likely cause of such feelings overwhelming her is her having no experience of being 'mothered', or emotionally cared for, as a child. She is left with no 'role model' to give her any confidence and does not feel that she has been sufficiently 'mothered' herself.

Usually all these emotional responses of mothers to their babies are highly visible. I witnessed this long ago when I chose to spend time in an Infant Welfare clinic. This was because I thought at the time that many children were referred 'too late' to the Child Guidance clinic where I worked. The mother/child relationship was already damaged and this should have been recognised earlier.

The type of 'Insecure Attachment' just described tends to leave the child to grow up with very low self-esteem and extreme doubts about finding 'anything good out there' being available to them. They tend to feel disappointed and have expectations of 'being let down'. These expectations in turn tend to help to bring it about. If you listen to such people when adults, they are likely to say such things as: 'I never was much good at anything', or 'I never seem to find a friend or partner who stays'. They often carry a constant feeling that people will not like them. Their sense of security tends to come from 'turning away' from any new experience, not expecting to find a good relationship with anyone. This leaves them with varying levels of anger and a sense of injustice, or a deep, long-lasting despair. This type of 'Insecure Attachment' is described as 'Insecure Avoidant'.

The second category of 'Insecure Attachment' comes about when the 'care givers' may well be able to offer some 'Secure Attachment' at times, but this is so variable and, as far as the child is concerned, so unpredictable, that he or she remains constantly confused. Such children spend their time trying to work out what will please their 'care givers' and make her, or him, available. They will scrutinise faces and constantly feel anxious about what will make her 'go away' again into this 'unavailable place'. This type of 'Insecure Attachment' leaves the adult chronically uncertain about themselves.

Although they have experienced being valued, they tend to continue to have difficulties in 'reading the signs' of others, misinterpreting their remarks or behaviour. Such people often do very well in particular aspects of their lives, if they have had encouraging messages and support in one area in particular. This might be in regard to their schooling or occasionally, for boys, their 'manliness' – being tough and strong. For girls, it may be that they get praise and affection for their appearance, or being subservient and well behaved. But, in general, such people continue to strive for approval, yet they may feel uncertain how to get it, except in their 'approved' ways. They also tend to be over ready to 'put things right', sometimes even taking inappropriate responsibility for things that go wrong. Such people tend to get very downcast if their attempts to please fail. This category of 'Insecure Attachment' is defined as 'Insecure Ambivalent'.

One of the saddest situations that can arise from this particular 'Insecure Attachment' is when a child feels unable to leave home because they have insufficient 'sense of self' to do so. In striving to feel safely 'Attached', they have got sucked into meeting the emotional needs of one of their parents. This is most likely to happen when a parent is on their own with an only child. The worst outcome is when their deep neediness, experienced by both of them, leads to the child growing up caring for their parent in their old age until their death. The daughter or son have by then long passed the age of having a family of their own, or even imagining that they could get that close to anyone else. I think that many people have met or know of someone in that situation; it is not that rare.

The third category of 'Insecure Attachment' was the last to be recognised as one needing a category of its own. Fortunately it occurs relatively rarely, but it gets the most publicity in the Press because its results tend to be the most traumatic. An example of this kind of 'Insecure Attachment' is extreme violent behaviour resulting in strong condemnation from the public, generally with little understanding of the possible causes. It tends to occur when 'care givers' are not only completely unable to give their children any care, but abuse them, either physically, with extremes of severity and often unpredictably or emotionally. Sometimes such abuses are presented as 'good' for the child.

For many today it is most likely to be sexual abuse, either of their own children, or those of close relatives. These ways of behaving arise out of their chaotic lifestyles. Many of them will have been abused themselves. This leaves their children terrified, confused and too often with no one they can trust to turn to. Some children, particularly as they get older, may be deeply fearful of the outcome if they do 'tell' about what is going on. They fear that they will not be believed, in spite of a recent improvement in attitudes in this respect. A greater fear is that they will be seen as responsible for the 'break-up' of the family and be punished even further. The result of children experiencing this type of treatment from the adults who should be caring for them can be extremely disruptive behaviour. It may make some children feel unable to go to school, run away from home, or have a desperate wish to do so.

This can equally apply if the so-called 'care' comes from an institution, where the abuse may well be a repetition of the child's previous experience. In this situation the sense of having 'nobody to turn to' may feel even worse. In adulthood, such people may seek a close relationship while rather young, in the hope of finding the love and security that they have never had. It is for this reason it will almost inevitably fail. For the same reason they will be totally unable to relate to any babies that may be the outcome of the failed relationship. A typical example of this is the young woman who gives birth again and again, only to have her babies removed by Social Services. There is no support service that can provide the 24/7 type of emotional and practical support she would need. Some of the support agencies that came near to this level, some years ago, have closed down, due to lack of funding. Many adults who have experienced this chaotic type of 'Insecure Attachment' become drug addicts or alcoholics, incapable of work. They may become suicidal, seeing this as the only way out of their sense of utter despair.

Others may respond quite differently, with men in particular becoming violent, leading them to being labelled 'indifferent' to the feelings of others, 'brutal' or 'callous'. It almost always leads to a prison sentence, which frequently leads to a further deterioration of their lives. Another result may be that such children, especially when they reach their teens, are labelled 'mentally ill' with schizophrenia, or suffering from a 'personality disorder'. On very rare occasions this can lead to a complete fragmenting of personalities.

For those who get to a psychiatric hospital, they may these days have only a relatively short stay and then be held in the community under a 'Treatment Order' requiring them to take their prescribed medication. If they fail to do this, they will be back in hospital. Bowlby defined this type of 'Insecure Attachment' as 'Insecure Disorganised'.

BOWLBY'S RECOGNITION OF OUR PRIMARY INSTINCTIVE DRIVE FOR ATTACHMENT

Dr. Bowlby was the first analyst to give recognition to our Attachment needs being our **Primary Instinctive drive, as it provides our sense of security.** In this respect he disagreed with Freud who considered that there were only two Instinctive Drives, for food and sex. Bowlby never doubted the important roles of these two drives, for physical survival and to maintain the species. But he and other Attachment theorists worked to gather evidence that clearly showed in animals, as well as humans, that our basic sense of security (that we need in order to function well in our environment) comes largely through our 'Attachments' to the people who care for us in our early years. This 'sense of security' can change as the years go by, either getting worse or better, according to our experiences.

Dr. Bowlby took ten years to complete his 'Theory of Attachment'. It was originally written in three separate books: 'Attachment', 'Separation' and 'Loss'. They have been available in one volume for a long time. Many people find this book hard to read as it is very detailed in its descriptions of all the research that he and others carried out. Bowlby was an inspired lecturer and two of his books which came later are easier to read: 'The Making and Breaking of Affectional Bonds', 1979 Tavistock and 'A Secure Base', 1988 Routledge. The latter is of particular relevance to therapists.

SECTION TWO

THE CREATING OF 'NEUROTIC SOLUTIONS'

I started section one of this short booklet by plunging the reader into a description of a basic principle of Attachment Theory, that is, describing 'Secure' and 'Insecure Attachments' and some generalisations about their outcomes. This is because, working over many years as an Attachment psychotherapist, I came to coin the phrase 'Neurotic Solutions', that I first wrote about in my book 'Understanding Ourselves', 1988 Macmillan. I needed a straightforward description of the deepest conflicts that arise within us, as we strive to maintain our original and highly individual 'Attachment Patterns', however distressing they may be. These patterns of 'Attachment', 'Secure' and 'Insecure', with some descriptions of their causes and outcomes, need to be understood before moving on to the more complex 'Neurotic Solutions' that I want to describe in far greater detail in the next two sections.

I believe that we are all engaged with the conflict inside our particularly personal 'Neurotic Solutions', whether we are aware of it or not. Other people's 'Neurotic Solutions' are much easier to recognise than one's own!

THE CREATING OF 'NEUROTIC SOLUTIONS'

At this point a clearer description of the meaning of the phrase 'Neurotic Solution' needs to be made. It is best understood in terms of a child's often desperate attempt to stay Attached to their 'care givers' at whatever cost. This is because this is essential for their survival. The child acts out their 'solution', as they see it, in their own highly individual situation. Some may fight the demands they feel are being expected of them. Such children, and later as adults, may be seen as 'difficult' or 'aggressive', which inevitably leaves them feeling even more unfairly rejected. Others express this sense of deprivation of love and care by being 'helpless' or ill and sometimes acting out their 'suffering' in the vain hope that this will lead to their getting the very love and care that they so desperately seek. Others will try and 'fit in' with the demands they feel they have to meet. This is often at great cost and gives them a sense of ultimate failure, as they attempt to fulfil the demands of their 'care givers' to be the special/successful/beautiful/clever person the child (and too often later, the adult) feels they must prove themselves to be. Sadly, some children reject any need to be deeply Attached to anyone, as the safest 'Neurotic Solution'. This can produce long-lasting problems as they grow older, finding it so fearful to make close intimate relationships as adults.

The biggest problem with all these 'Neurotic Solutions' is the fact that they are being built up as a form of response to the 'care giver's' expectations or demands. The child is not consciously aware at the time of what they are doing. It just feels like a 'way of being' over which they feel they have no choice. It feels like a way they 'have to be'. Such people always carry with them a sense of injustice, anger or the deepest sense of loss and sadness.

THE DEPTH OF SUFFERING WITHIN THE 'NEUROTIC SOLUTION'

By steering away from the theories of previous analysts and deeply questioning the limitations of the medical psychiatric categories, Bowlby has provided us with a far more realistic, understandable and hopeful way of both perceiving and treating much human distress. Over the years, I have come to understand and recognise what a large part of therapy is spent on working on the 'Neurotic Solutions'. This involves the person concerned, not only recognising them, but coming to fully understand how they operate, often in disguised form. Above all, I have become most interested in why some people suffer so much from feeling driven to maintain their original patterns of thought and behaviour, however painful they may be. Yet, for these people, letting such perceptions 'go', feels impossible and, for some, like a terrible risk, too great even to contemplate.

At this stage it seems important to explain why I chose the phrase 'Neurotic Solution' to help people who feel so stuck in their painful patterns, to make sense of them. The word 'neurotic' is so often used derogatively. It simply means suffering from some form of conflict at a level of which the person may, or may not, be aware. They rarely understand the connections between their original experiences and their current feelings and behaviour. This in itself adds to their stress. If they are aware of having very mixed feelings, they generally experience a sense of them being 'out of their control'. This is often described by the person feeling it as if the anxiety or depression, or particular action, 'comes out of the blue'! It feels as if it is 'outside themselves', created by other forces. This is why it is so easy for them to feel someone else must 'put it right', or something else will 'take it away' or at least ease it, like a pill, a drink, going away somewhere different. But for most people it comes from being aware that there are others who do not feel the same as they do. This leaves them feeling perplexed as to why some people can do things apparently easily, while to them they feel so impossible. Some may then recognise a sense of 'unreality' about their fears, which may add to their sense of confusion.

Claustrophobia

To take a very simple example, some people feel terrified of being in a confined space. They cannot face going through an M.R.I scan or, even for some, getting into a lift. At such times they may become very conscious that to others, it is 'ordinary' and produces no feelings of panic or terror at all. Most people know the word claustrophobia and what it means, but, for those who suffer from it, the inability to do these things feels absolute.

Luckily, for those suffering in this way, most big shops and stations now have open escalators, so these and other options make it possible for them to avoid their fears. But it is not without pain, as such people often feel shame or some sense of embarrassment about it. Some people may go to great lengths to hide their fear, but claustrophobia is so common that it has recently become easier for such people to expose their fear more publicly.

Recently a well known TV doctor showed in quite a matter of fact way that at the last minute he could not face an MRI scan arranged as part of his programme. Although this was obviously not planned, it seemed to me a good contribution, enabling doctors to be seen to have the same problems as some of their patients.

Agoraphobia

Those who suffer from the opposite fear, known as agoraphobia, are left feeling unable to go out. This can have far more serious consequences as it can leave people feeling trapped at home. This leaves them unable to go to work, or do ordinary things like shopping or even walking down the road to post a letter. Such people are often keenly aware of a deep wish to be able to go out and about, but cannot cope with the level of terror they feel at the prospect of doing so. More women suffer from this than men, and it is not that unusual in children. They used to be described as 'School Refusers'. It took some time before the recognition came that some of these children were not always scared of what might happen to them at school, but that they were frightened about what might happen at home, in their absence. This might be a fear that a parent had gone, or one parent was hurt by another, or even a younger sibling come to harm. Because of the sense of 'being different' and feeling generally less willing to expose this problem, many agoraphobics will try and hide this fear, lessening the conflict by a combination of accepting a restricted life, or only going out with someone very close to them.

If such people live alone, it may be that the agoraphobic fears provide a hope that at last someone will come and show them that they do care about them and rescue them from their original early experience of isolation and fear. All these neurotic fears have their origins in early childhood experiences. They reappear at some later stage, if a similar situation arises, leaving the person resorting to their original 'solution' to try and regain some sense of themselves. The saddest fact is that no 'Neurotic Solution' ever gives the person the good feelings they are seeking.

This kind of situation held within a couple can sometimes allow both partners to be unaware of the real 'power dynamic' that is going on between them. The 'power' feelings, even if only dimly recognised, may lie with the helpless 'scared one' who 'makes' the other take them out. Or it may be more consciously held by the one who maintains the other's dependence on them. Some sufferers will find the courage to seek help, but this is often hard to find. Unfortunately such help, when found, is unlikely to encourage the person to think about when these feelings may have started, or why they feel so hard to change. The most difficult part for the person concerned, and the most uncomfortable, may well be to explore the conflict at the centre of it. It is the 'Neurotic Solution' which contains the drive **to stay trapped and feel unable to go out alone** in order to try and get some feeling of being 'in control' of the person who is with them. In this way they attempt to ease the current feelings of anxiety, set off by some memories of how they felt when very small. This can happen even if the person is not consciously aware of the memory at the time.

THE RETURN OF THE REPRESSED

Freud provided us with a very useful theory, which he described as 'The Return of the Repressed'. For some people, on hearing this, they understandably turn away from it, as it sounds too difficult to decipher! What it means is simply that, in our efforts to find a 'solution' to our emotional pain, without being aware of it, we behave in ways that bring about the very feelings that we are trying to escape from!

This is most clearly seen when people take to alcohol, hoping to feel 'better' as described earlier, but landing up with their money gone, their self-esteem lowered and their very closest partners and friends rejecting them. This outcome applies to so many ways in which people behave. To look at another example: people who eat more than they need try to comfort themselves from feeling a sense of having some deep 'need' that they do not know how to meet. It may be experienced as a great 'emptiness' that needs filling. If this sense of need is met by food, which the person does not actually need, it tends to make them feel worse: their favourite clothes may no longer fit, they often feel more exhausted and less agile.

I once listened to a woman in her thirties who had three children of school age. She would set aside a day to bake for them, making breads, cakes and biscuits. When she had finished, she was overcome with a desire to eat some. At this point in her story she started to cry, but managed to say, hiding her face, that she couldn't stop and went on eating more and more until only a small amount was left. For a brief moment she looked at me in fear, as if she was expecting a condemnation of such behaviour. Before I could say anything, she produced an outpouring of how 'greedy' she was, how ashamed she felt, and guilty and 'wicked' for depriving her children of the food she had cooked for them. Within five minutes of being with me she had shared what was at the heart of her conflict: the strong desire to be a loving mother, making something lovely for her children, and then acting in a way that made her feel a 'wicked' mother, depriving them of her love, at the same time betraying her own desperate need to feel the love for herself.

Some people feel the opposite of this, as they have a great fear of eating. This often leads them to lose so much weight that only at the beginning are they able to hide what they are doing. This condition, known as anorexia in its extreme form, is also known about by most people. It can be very serious. A lesser known condition, that brings great distress too, is known as bulimia, when the person eats, indeed they have to, in order to go through the process that they feel driven to do. This is to vomit up the food they have eaten. The sense of having to 'get rid of something' inside themselves is their 'Neurotic Solution', but it gives them such a brief sense of relief. Those that I have known have all been women. They have shared how they felt about it, describing their sense of disgust with themselves, again confirming their own feelings of being 'unworthy'. They tend to reject themselves out of hand and put themselves down, by constantly over-elevating others. Their conflict is exposed when they react very sensitively to anyone else criticising them and by their feeling so helpless to change their behaviour. This would require them to openly acknowledge they are valuable, loveable people, just as good as anyone else. But this is often too hard for them to do.

There are many common examples of people's fears, such as having to give a speech, or even speak at all, for example at a farewell works party, at a wedding, or, for many the hardest thing of all, at a funeral of a close family member or friend. Others may feel terrified at going into a crowded room where there is nobody that they know. For others it can feel utterly impossible to go off on their own for a holiday, especially if they have had the recent loss of a very close, long-term Attachment figure.

These types of fears are variable, some seeming 'absolute', virtually for all time. Others may be perceived as hopefully changeable: if they can be understood as a 'Neurotic Solution', and the person can discover how to discard them. Quite differently, it may be that a period of time allows the person to recover sufficiently from their sense of loss, to regain their confidence and overcome their fear. Most people need help and support to do so. If in fact it is fulfilling a need for a 'Neurotic Solution', these can change too, if another version of the 'Neurotic Solution' works 'better'. This will not be due to a conscious decision, but rather a measure of how desperate their need is, particularly if they are unaware of it. This will be true if they find another way of 'feeling safer'. To give an example, some men who feel very insecure and fear their wives may leave them, may start by appearing very jealous and demanding to know all the time who they are with, or where they are. This may not solve their neurotic need to feel 'safely in control' of their wife, so they will change that 'solution' to another one, demanding that she goes nowhere without him.

This kind of behaviour, especially if it escalates, is another perfect example of 'The Return of the Repressed', as the very way he has chosen to 'secure his wife', may drive her to leave, unless she feels trapped, and feels she has nowhere else to go.

THE SOURCE OF STRENGTH WITHIN THE DRIVE FOR ATTACHMENT

At the risk of seeming repetitive, I want to stress again that these feelings of fear and anger and desolation are so **strong and persistent**, for some people in particular, because being 'attached' is our **primary instinctive drive**. These words in themselves need to make sense to the individual concerned. 'Primary' just means the most important, the one that counts above all others. This is because the definition of 'instinctive' means our 'survival' depends on it.

We tend to think of our needs of survival in bodily terms, in the sense of needing firstly air, then water and food and an appropriate temperature and some reliable shelter. But this is why the word 'primary' does make sense. I have worked with people who do at times feel momentarily that they cannot breathe. Such a person feels as if there is 'no air' for them. Others feel such depths of despair that they turn away from nourishment, finding it hard to eat and to sleep. Those who feel extreme anxiety sometimes feel hot nearly all the time, bothered by sweating, which tends to make them more anxious. Others, for their own reasons, may feel the opposite, constantly cold and a bit shivery. A sense of feeling that they have no safe 'shelter' is commonly felt by children: if they feel that their 'care givers' do not want them in the home, or constantly criticise them, or ignore them. For all of us, our capacity to provide these things for ourselves, or to know how to obtain them, largely depends on our state of mind. (I am not of course referring here to the circumstances of someone in a war zone, or who has been rendered by outside forces to be helpless.)

For those who have had a sufficiently 'Secure Attachment' their feelings in general will be very different from those who have not. They will tend to feel in general calm and confident in a normal way, not over-confident, nor frequently lacking it. They will feel able to cope with experiences of loss rather differently. They will meet changes in their situation, like a new school or new job, moving home, or losing a friend, with emotional upset in varying degrees, but will have an expectation that there will be enough support around them to help them to cope. This will apply even when severe losses occur, like the loss of a lifelong partner. They will work through the grieving process slowly and recover enough of a sense of their own value to regain, with support, an ability to find a way to adapt to their new circumstances.

UNWILLING LOSS OF ATTACHMENT

Bowlby considered it is the **unwilling** loss of an Attachment that is the source of all our deepest emotional disturbances. This grieving for such losses is currently receiving a lot of public attention. This is happening literally as I write, because two royal figures have felt able to break the usual 'Royal Protocol' and talk openly about how long their feelings of loss have lasted following the death of their mother. They felt previously that these could not be openly expressed because of their position. This openness is especially important in the sense that both figures are men, and for so many men to talk about their feelings is equated with being 'weak'.

They are not the first royals to do this. Long ago an uncrowned king gave up his future crown as he was prepared to admit he could not cope with its immense responsibilities without his chosen 'Attachment figure' by his side. Another young royal boy, caught up in the disaster that killed Earl Mountbatten, which also resulted in the death of the boy's twin, wrote fully and courageously about this unique loss. He too wrote about the equally grave consequences of feeling obliged to keep quiet for many years about his feelings. He recovered as a result of making a lifelong friendship with another lone twin, having some psychotherapy, and he ultimately felt able to marry happily and have a family.

The current two royals, assisted by the wife of one of them, have started a group to help others with so called 'mental problems' through training in long distance running. It is a known fact that exercise helps people to feel less depressed and anxious, due to chemical changes that take place in the brain when exercising. But perhaps what the group is less aware of is that joining others engaged in the same activity tends to make for a sense of 'belonging'. In this way they not only gain a feeling of achievement, increasing their sense of worth, but they feel part of a group to which they are 'Attached', caring about each other, the more confident ones spreading that sense among the others. I believe that for some young people who have had the experience of their family splitting up, especially when they are very young, this can affect them for life.

ADOLESCENCE

Dr. Bowlby stressed the importance of recognising that most severe emotional disturbances are due to experiences in early childhood. But he also emphasised the important stage of adolescence as a time when equally severe damage can occur. He also added a very optimistic note, as he based this view on the fact that adolescence is such a huge drawn-out stage of change, physically and emotionally. Because of this, patterns of quite severe emotional disturbance may newly occur. But if a new opportunity arises through a complete change of environment – this may be at college or at work – it may bring young people into contact with skilled, mature and supportive mentors.

One boy who was frequently bullied at school and scorned as a 'wimp' later got into an apprenticeship scheme. He discovered there that he had skills with machinery that he had no idea were within him. He won an award and the change in him was very marked. This is not to say his early experiences no longer affected him at all, but he was able to build a much truer perception of himself, rather than the one both the school bullies gave him and which his father endorsed. He did this by simply telling his son constantly 'you must stand up for yourself' and 'act like a man'. As there was a gang of six older boys who bullied him in his school, with no staff intervention, he felt utterly alone with no one to turn to for help.

When listening to these sorts of accounts, it is important for the therapist to hear fully how each individual personally responds, and not jump to conclusions. This boy hardly ever spoke openly against his father's treatment of him, or dared tell him how he felt. When he did show his feelings, it would be in the form of shrugging his shoulders. He was able to express far deeper feelings of anger towards his mother. He felt sure she was 'letting him down' by not intervening, but then softened this by saying that he knew she was scared of his dad too. It seemed he felt she should have protected him, as she was the only one who gave him any sense of security. This was the very reason why he could express his anger towards her, daring to believe she loved him enough not to retaliate.

THE HIDDEN SENSE OF POWER WITHIN THE 'NEUROTIC SOLUTION'

The sense of power that makes most people feel good, as Jean Baker Miller wrote many times, is not the kind that is 'power over', which requires someone else to be 'powerless', but the kind of power that enables others to develop and feel more confident in themselves. Examples of this come from the way most parents treat their children when they care about them and support them. It also comes from the relations between teachers and pupils in a similar creative environment. This occurs when teachers are able to recognise that some of their pupils may well surpass them and feel pleased and proud of this. Such teachers never have to bully or humiliate their pupils.

It has become very clear to me that an 'illusion of power' lies at the heart of every 'Neurotic Solution', taking the form of a 'campaign' which can sometimes be maintained for many years. This illusion can often be so well disguised that it becomes hard to recognise. It is an expression by the person concerned of an attempt to maintain some valuation of themselves, however painful and distorted this version may be. To give some examples: one of the most common is a determination by someone to deny any form of feeling 'good' about themselves. They demonstrate that

they can do without this. Whatever their achievements may be, they will not allow themselves any credit for them. This is done in an attempt to show that they can live without the love which was originally given to them. Sometimes people feel driven to be ill, or helpless, in order to **force** someone to take care of them at last. Another person may endlessly express their depressed and anxious feelings, saying they 'want to make **the whole world know'** of their emotional deprivation as a small child, believing this will lead to their being rescued in some way and **force** their mother to recognise what she has done.

The man who said he was 'going to make a bomb to kill the queen' was stating a huge need to **retaliate** for his belief that his treatment was due to the shape of his nose, that he could never escape from, that portrayed him as a 'foreigner'. Another man, who had a violent, sadistic father, wanted '**to blow up** the whole world'. Nothing less would equate with the terror he felt that he had been made to endure.

When such feelings are expressed and shared, with a real understanding of their origin being an expression of a **deep feeling of loss**, they make sense to the person concerned. Gradually such a response, especially when it has been strengthened and maintained over many years, can be recognised, sadly, as fruitless. The worst aspect of these 'Neurotic Solutions' is that they tend to bar such people even further from feeling valued or good about themselves. They need to be recognised as expressing the depth of pain that some 'Insecure Attachments' bring in their wake.

GIRLS IN RELATION TO FATHER FIGURES

This issue commonly occurs when, for example, girls or young women feel forced to meet the sexual demands of a male member of the family, or, as has frequently happened in the past, a male 'boss' at work who had power over them. The need to escape from this sense of being trapped and helpless has been briefly referred to in the description of some 'Insecure Disorganised Attachments'. In this situation, the girl has a vague sense of the 'power' she holds to divulge, or not to divulge, what is going on. This conflict may be at a level of constant awareness, or it may be only fleeting, but it always holds a sense of frightening confusion. If she does not divulge what is going on out of fear of the consequences, this produces a 'Neurotic Solution' which can affect her for the rest of her life. It may lead to such an uncertain 'sense of self' that she feels unable ever to risk being in a 'powerful' position in the future. For example, she may refuse to take on a more responsible post at work, as she fears the anger that may be directed at her being in a potentially 'powerful' position. Alternatively it may produce the opposite type of feeling and behaviour, so that she acts out the 'power over others', either in her home or in her workplace. She then finds herself suffering from being intensely disliked. This is another example of the 'Return of the Repressed', when the 'bullied' becomes the 'bully'. If such a person has an opportunity to resolve the conflict enough, through a therapeutic intervention in which she is fully engaged, she can reach a stable position of increased empathy and have a genuine wish to help others in any powerless position.

BOYS WHO ARE ENTANGLED WITH THEIR MOTHERS

Boys caught up in very close relationships with their mothers can sometimes have their father's fears of this relationship lead to jealous feelings and anger that threatens their son. This leaves him feeling a threat to his father. In this way he holds 'the power' over both parents. The confusion arising from these conflicts can lead to long-term anxieties about authoritative figures in his later life. He tends to experience them as having power over him. In turn, as his sexual fantasies towards his mother lie in the area of being 'forbidden', this provides a particularly distorted form of 'Insecure Attachment'. It makes it hard for him not to continue devaluing himself by feeling driven into an inability to recognise that his real security lies in an adult, loving relationship when it is available. This too often produces a very common fear among men about 'sexual failure'. They tend to perceive sex solely in terms of *their own sexual performance.* In the most extreme form, it can lead to such boys in later life becoming fearful of whether they can meet the sexual desires of their partners. When they do, their thoughts will take the form immediately of believing 'they won't be able to do it again'! This maintains their 'Neurotic Solution', that is, the perception that to be sexual with someone they really love is not actually available to them.

POWER FEELINGS WITHIN REVENGE

Another commonly held sense of 'power' is held at different levels of the person's awareness. The fantasies such people express about what they would 'like to do' to their 'care givers', who they feel have been the cause of their years of suffering, can be extremely violent. People who express such ideas very rarely carry them out in reality. Quite often their early 'care givers' are no longer around, or their whereabouts are unknown. They may even be dead, but the fantasies can sometimes remain for a long time.

THE EXPERIENCE OF RENT BOYS

I once was invited to listen to the accounts of some young men (with their agreement) as an observer at a very unusual type of Therapy Centre. They were young men who, as boys, had run away from 'children's homes'. They had been placed there because of the breakdown of their original homes. They had all got to London where they were 'picked up' and used as 'rent boys'. One of them spoke of how he was 'passed around' between a number of different men whose real names were hidden by 'pet names'. He said he soon realised some of them were well known public figures. By the time he had the freedom to try and identify them, from their faces in newspapers, or voices on television, he believed that naming them in court would never stand up to the kind of scrutiny he would have to face there.

I left the session recognising just how defeated these young men felt. This experience added to my deep interest and concern about the cause of these older men's need to act so powerfully over others. I wondered if changes in the law with regard to homosexuality have played any part in lessening these cruel behaviours. They certainly continue in some religious groups where enforced celibacy exists.

MEN'S VIOLENCE TOWARDS WOMEN

Violence by men towards women has only relatively recently been seen as a shameful and outrageously frequent event in our society. It takes so many forms: sexual, physical and psychological. Stalking, which has caused many women severe anxiety over a number of years, has only recently been acknowledged as a criminal offence.

NO CONSENSUS ABOUT THE CAUSE OF THE 'NEED FOR POWER OVER OTHERS'.

There seems to be no general agreed understanding about what causes this need to be 'powerful over others'. It has gone on largely unchecked, and in many societies accepted as the norm. I believe it arises out of unacknowledged deep feelings of helplessness and fear. For so many generations men have been brought up to deny any feelings about being rejected or abandoned. A large proportion of men in this country who hold the highest positions have been to Public Schools. They have been sent away from their parents, homes and everything familiar to them at the age of eight. This separation at such an early age is the price they have to pay for having the most highly sought after and most expensive education in an environment that has rigid power structures, both between the boys and between the boys and the masters.

Other huge separations, such as the one when many children were incorrectly described as 'orphans' and sent off to Australia, have been recognised in retrospect as a cause of great emotional damage. The same applied to many small children sent away from home during their evacuation from cities during the last war.

Perhaps it is time to recognise that every form of early separation of children from Attachment Figures is highly likely to cause severe emotional pain. I think that our society pays a heavy price for failing to fully recognise this.

In the next section, I want to describe how far more complicated 'Neurotic Solutions' play themselves out and the highly individual way they are experienced by those suffering from them.

SECTION THREE

AWARENESS OF THE THREE ASPECTS OF THE MIND

Most people who are sufficiently aware of their own emotional state will recognise when conflicting feelings are causing them distress. These may be slight, short-term and relatively easily resolved, or may be intense and long-term. If the latter is the case, this sense of how the person would 'like to be' and how in some sense they feel 'driven to be', can bring about awareness of another part of their mind. This may be so vague it is hardly sensed at all. If it is experienced, it can feel like an 'ineffective observer', unable to resolve the acute conflict between the two sides, which for so many people seems to have been felt, particularly at first, as beyond reach.

This type of deeply embedded 'Neurotic Solution', felt to be unchangeable by the sufferer, is always unique to that person. It is based on their highly individual experience within their family and how they interpret it. This has left them with a sense of unchangeable suffering and at the same time a concept of the life they could have, if they were free of the pain. This idea was described by one client as 'seeing life through pink-tinted spectacles', as it felt so far away at that time.

Experiences within the same family can be so different for its individual members. This often explains why one child may grow up to be very emotionally disturbed and others in the same family will not. Even so, there are certain characteristics within all 'Neurotic Solutions' that come from 'Insecure Attachments'. These feel compulsive, seductive and very persistent. For many people who experience them, they can feel as if they 'take over' a large part of their life. Those people generally find ways of maintaining their 'Neurotic Solutions' without being aware of what they are doing. This is quite simply because they feel driven to stay with the 'Neurotic Solution' that they have come to feel is both 'how' and 'who' they are. **This is the version of themselves that they got from their 'care givers' and that they have interpreted in their own individual way**. It always carries some sense of emotional pain.

In brief, the Third Part of Mind (the conscious-thinking part that **knows about** both ways of feeling) enables people to discover **how** to move from their 'Neurotic Solutions' (painful ways of thinking and feeling about themselves) to a more real way of being. It enables them to see how they have maintained their 'Neurotic Solutions', originally created in their childhood, in far more complicated and disguised versions in their adult life, re-creating their original emotional distress into the current version. This in turn finally helps them find the courage to move into a more realistic valuation of themselves.

TALKING ABOUT 'BOTH SIDES OF THE CONFLICT' – GOING FROM Z TO A

Those people who have experienced a period of feeling free of their suffering, either for long or very fleeting periods of time, seem to share much more similar words than those describing very individual experiences of their 'Neurotic Solutions'. The essential characteristic seems to be a sense of freedom. The other most commonly used expressions are of feeling 'calm', 'in control', 'peaceful', 'happy', even some deeper feelings like 'joy', and, with an apparent sense of disbelief, 'love'. When these sorts of experiences are described, the person becomes slightly more aware of the existence of the 'third part of mind' already referred to. This is because these feelings challenge the notions so strongly held within their 'Neurotic Solution' that 'to let them go' is impossible.

The two sides of the conflicting perceptions of themselves need to have been talked about at length. This means, in reality, hearing a great many stories about the pain and suffering, but generally very little about having any experience of being free of them. I have found it useful to find a shorthand way of referring to the 'two sides' of feeling, by using the letters 'A', standing for the concept of being free from that person's emotional pain, and 'Z' being the way to refer to all the painful variations of suffering they have described. I think this can only be done when the person is ready to feel that the therapist has really heard and shown some signs of truly understanding the full depth of their pain. It might otherwise seem a bit 'glib', rather than useful.

One thing that has often been expressed to me by people in long-term psychotherapy, is the sense of how much more 'awful' the 'Z' feelings seem to be after the person has experienced a period of 'A' feelings. These can often be described as 'worse than ever'. When I ask the person why they think it feels like that, they tend to say it feels so 'hard' to bear with all the pain again after a period of feeling 'so good'. I try at this stage to help the person not to be downcast at the thought that this is a 'relapse', as many psychiatrists describe a return of symptoms, but instead to see it as a 'backlash' by the 'Z' way of thinking, to prevent a further experience of an 'A' way. This is the 'Neurotic Solution' trying to regain its thinking pattern and to once again strengthen the notion that it cannot safely be changed.

Sometimes the person can be encouraged to see what may have occurred to bring the 'Z' pattern back again. I ask them to try and recall what they may have either been thinking about, or perhaps actually been doing, that could have 'triggered' the 'Z's' return. This can sometimes lead to an enormous new awareness of just what the 'Z' way of thinking is trying to make them believe about themselves.

PEOPLE'S VARYING AWARENESS OF THEIR 'NEUROTIC SOLUTIONS'

Some people never recognise that their behaviour is driven by their 'Neurotic Solution'. These behaviours often go unrecognised by their friends and stay numbingly difficult to understand by those who experience them. One woman wrote in her diary during her middle age how painful and embarrassing she found it that, for the two days before she ever had to set out on a journey away from home, she suffered from severe diarrhoea. She thought at first that it was due to facing a sea crossing, as she always suffered from sea sickness. She then wrote that this could not be the case, as she had experienced it just as badly on going up to Scotland. This was a woman who had, in her early days, been so frightened of the 'suitors' who came bearing flowers to the door that she begged her sister to 'send them away'. She said she had no wish to get married. As it turned out, she spent her life at home taking her mother's place when she died, taking over the care of her father. She ran his extensive household with great efficiency, managed a number of servants and important events and held an unpaid, but prestigious, post of her own. She made no further attempts to travel long distances. She would not have wished to gain any sort of further insight into her feelings as such an idea would have been rejected, except through prayer, as she was a deeply religious person who strongly disparaged psychology.

Another woman of a similar age, but a different era, described her compulsive drive to steal from shops. She was relatively well off, married and working. I first listened to her story in a probation office. It seemed that she was drawn to 'shoplifting', but only in large stores with franchises offering either elegant clothes or beautiful toiletries. She admitted that she could have paid for them herself. As is so often the case, one person's 'Neurotic Solution' also deeply affects the other people around her.

This woman was inevitably caught. She appeared in court and was treated by an enlightened type of judge, who put her on a probation order, with the threat that if she stole again it would be a prison sentence. She seemed to have no idea why she behaved in this way, but, as she spoke, it was apparent that she had a long-term, deep-seated feeling about being 'cheated' in some way. It felt obvious to me that there was a connection between these feelings and her behaviour. As she spoke in a distressed way, it seemed that she felt these clothes and beauty items were really 'hers'. Her story embodied a perfect example again of 'The Return of the Repressed', as she found all her old feelings about being the 'unloved', 'bad' member of the family were back with her more strongly than ever. She lost her job and many of her friends. I soon had to move on from this office, so I just hoped that the very knowledgeable probation officer would be able to help her regain a different perception of herself in due course.

A very different kind of person who also may be equally blind to the drive within his 'Neurotic Solution' is the man who acts out an apparent belief in his own sense of being of the utmost importance in whatever group he may be in. This may be a club, a community, or even at work. Such people tend to give out a strong sense of being 'superior' to anyone else and, most of all, of being indispensable. If this view is strongly challenged, or they lose the position that is helping them to maintain this belief, they may be at risk, through having deeply hidden from themselves a sense of their fear of frailty or helplessness, which leaves them open to this type of exposure. If this happens suddenly, or very publicly, it can lead to them becoming depressed or physically ill.

THE MEDICAL MODEL

One man's story was told to me by a sympathetic relative. It seems that he held a very prestigious well paid job. When he was suddenly made redundant he found himself unable to do anything at home. He was soon referred to a psychiatrist via his GP. He was then admitted to a psychiatric hospital and treated with very strong drugs. He was described as having had a 'nervous breakdown'. He was eventually sent home, but soon became worse and was readmitted under 'section'. He is now at home, but unable to go to work. It seems that, in summary, he had a history that left him feeling permanently inferior to his older brother in the eyes of his mother. When this prestigious job came so abruptly to an end, he was completely unable to cope with his change of circumstances. He lost his 'sense of self' that depended, without him realising it, on his status at work which met his mother's approval.

What happens so often in the 'Medical Model', is an absence of any real attempt to help the person to recognise how and why it is that what has happened to them lies at the heart of their condition. They may be offered very short-term counselling of

'Cognitive Behaviour Therapy'. This may help people who have a short-term response to some recent incident in their lives. It rarely helps those with deep-seated patterning that has lasted all their lives, of which they may be largely unaware. This can leave them at risk, when their 'Neurotic Solution' fails them. (In the case of this man, the need of a prestigious job to keep him Attached to his mother.) They then remain at risk of being labelled 'mentally ill' unless they can get some more long-term type of psychotherapy that can enable them to discover a different, less fragile 'sense of self'.

I do not wish to be seen as 'writing off' the 'Medical Model', far from it. At times it may be very important for a psychiatrist with medical knowledge to diagnose a variety of possible neurological conditions, that otherwise could easily be missed. There also may well be times when a short course of antidepressants actually helps someone to recover enough to use psychotherapy. There are times as well when a psychotherapist's client may be suicidal and a psychiatric 'back-up' is essential. I believe what is needed is for psychiatrists to work fully with psychotherapists, or to have a psychotherapy training themselves.

DIFFICULTIES IN TALKING ABOUT EMOTIONAL PAIN

It is no wonder that many people shy away from the very idea of talking to a psychotherapist. Bowlby was one of the few psychiatrists who well understood this, saying how daunting it can feel to many people to bring back those early painful memories. It is only when a high level of suffering, combined with the hope that some long lasting relief may be found, is experienced that some people will be driven to seek psychotherapy.

Some people hardly know how to begin to 'tell their story'. I believe that this may not only be due to a cause already mentioned, of people being unused to exploring their own feelings, but also of having had some very severe experiences at a pre-verbal stage of their lives. In this situation they literally do not have the words to describe their experiences. This does not mean that they have no memories of these experiences. They may come from very early physical or sexual abuse, or they may be largely emotional, experienced as a deep sense of loss of the kind that follows the death or departure of a parent at a very early stage of the child's life long before they are able to verbalise their feelings or thoughts.

HELPFUL USE OF METAPHOR, OR SIMILE

I became particularly interested in this form of pre-verbal memory as it affects many twins who have lost their twin, either at birth or during the few years after. Children up to the ages of three or four years old may have a good idea of what is going on around them, but little ability to put their responses into words. As a result of that, many adults behave as though small children are deaf and do not understand anything about what is being said in their hearing! As adults, such people may struggle to describe their feelings and, in these situations, I always suggest that they try and describe them in a form of metaphor or even simile. It often leads them to all sorts of freedoms to speak and say such things as feeling 'only a half', said by many lone twins for example. This feeling can be used to describe that sense of loss not just by twins who have lost a twin in adult life, but by those whose loss was very early.

Many other vivid descriptions of feelings begin to emerge, such as, 'it is like 'carrying a dead weight'; 'I'm living in a black cloud.'

Most people have heard of Mr Churchill's 'Black Dog' reference to his feelings of being depressed.

BODILY EXPRESSIONS OF PREVERBAL MEMORY

Recently, I listened to a lone twin who had lost her twin just before birth. She is in therapy with a particular therapist who works almost entirely in terms of the effects on the body of early loss. She was describing her 'memories' in terms of 'rushing water' and of 'waterfalls'. These feelings are so vivid to the person concerned, but to talk about them is really hard, as they fear most people will write it all off as 'crazy'.

Dr. Siegal, one of the world's experts in the functioning of the brain and its development, describes this form of foetal memory as 'implicit', as distinct from the ordinary use of the word 'memory', (of the kind involved in knowing what we had for breakfast) which he described as 'explicit'. I think that distinguishing between the two is very important. Dr. Louis Cozolino, a neuropsychotherapist who exchanged an email with me on the subject, believes this kind of 'implicit' memory can start during the third trimester of pregnancy. He thought from his research that such memories could well be 're-activated' or in some sense brought to conscious recognition if an event of a similar kind reoccurred in later life. He thought it would come in a similar non verbal form.

I would like at this point to share with readers that I had such an experience myself last autumn that came as a complete surprise. I had sat alone with my younger brother until he died in his home early in the morning. I watched his breathing finally stop. He had played a particularly important part in my life after my identical twin sister died, when we were three years old. As I sat down, having got up to confirm that my brother had died, I experienced a feeling that was entirely in my body, which I neither could, nor needed to, verbalise. Now that I am trying to do so, it felt like a great 'swoosh' of energy that rushed out of my body, with his going. I was utterly taken aback by it. I made no attempt to understand it. It was simply a huge, bodily sensation that astonished me. I need just to add that it was not a 'religious' experience, as I am an agnostic, or a Humanist as I prefer to describe it.

It was some days later, when I had time and energy to think about it, that Cozolino's words came back to me. It seemed that my brother's death, because of our strong early closeness, did awaken an 'implicit' memory of my being told by my mother that my twin sister had died. I have never had any conscious memory of this event.

My older brother told me about his memory of it, a short time before he died. It seems he went at once and sat on my mother's lap and so I went to my father's. I guess that this information was too big and too complicated for me to respond to verbally. It seems possible that such a huge sense of loss may well have been experienced bodily, perhaps particularly as we were identical twins. I did feel this earlier loss held a response to more than my brother's departure from my life. It meant the end, not only of my Attachment to him, but also to my sister and my whole family, as I was then the last one alive.

I hope that including such a personal experience in this writing seems a proper experience to share, as I know how grateful I felt at understanding it, in a way that I would not have been able to do without Cozolino's willingness to share his knowledge with me. I would like to think that others who may experience something similar will not be scared or nonplussed by it, but rather, instead, interested in thinking how it might be an 'implicit' memory for them.

'NEUROTIC SOLUTIONS' AND THEIR CONNECTION WITH PSYCHOSOMATIC SYMPTOMS

I believe that the description of 'psychosomatic' illnesses is misleading. It joins together the words 'psycho', which simply means of the mind, or emotions, with the word 'soma' which means 'of the body'. To put these two together seems to me superfluous. I cannot imagine feeling any strong emotion without it having some effect on my body. Equally, if I have a physical symptom, I have some kind of emotional response to it. For example, at a very simplistic level, even if I have a cold I can feel annoyed at not being able to go somewhere that I had been looking forward to!

I was very lucky to have the opportunity to do the first research study into what was called 'Psychosomatic Vaginitis'. This was carried out at Birmingham Brook Clinic and the VD clinic in the Birmingham General Hospital. Young women who came to Brook suffered pain and discomfort from very unpleasant vaginal symptoms of discharge and extreme soreness. One client who wrote her own account in 'Understanding Ourselves' described her symptoms as being impossible 'to sit down in comfort'. I was surprised at the time how many years some of the women had suffered their symptoms and how many had gone to their GPs and been given endless pessaries etc. without success.

This research was published in 'The Practitioner', a journal for GPs, as well as my writing about it more informally elsewhere. I am referring to it now as it was so obvious that most of the women were 'using' their symptoms to protect themselves from an impossible conflict. Put simply, they wanted to be sexual with part of themselves, but with another part, for all sorts of different reasons, they did not. To be 'unable to be sexual' because of an 'infection' was the 'Neurotic Solution'. When the bacterial report showed emphatically that there was no infection, most of these women were willing to examine gently the possible reasons why their bodies had produced symptoms that mimicked a real infection so convincingly. Once this idea was discussed in a relaxed atmosphere of complete confidence, both they and I were surprised by the speed at which these symptoms disappeared or greatly lessened. They all experienced, in different ways, a sense of loss. It also helped them to understand the reasons for any return of their symptoms.

I believe that some of the symptoms that we all suffer from carry some aspect of our own 'Neurotic Solution' without our necessarily being aware of it.

THE USE OF DREAMS IN PSYCHOTHERAPY

Having already described how helpful metaphor can be in therapy, and a recognition of the importance of understanding how we use our bodies to express our feelings, I want to move on to the use of dream material in a similar way.

Our dreams give us access to how our minds work when we are no longer 'censoring' them! Dreams are not of course limited to when we are asleep, though those dreams that people have in the day tend to have a different quality from night ones. When they are remembered, and some people are not able to record them, they give us some idea of how our unconscious mind is working. I believe this can sometimes be very helpful. If a client tells me a particularly vivid dream that they have had, I am always most reluctant to 'interpret' it to them. Instead, I would ask them for their understanding of it. One example of this came from a woman who was well aware of the conflict inside her 'Neurotic Solution'. She described how in her dream she was on holiday with her husband and she was on the beach with her back to the sea. She wanted to go up the steeply sloped beach to where they were staying. As she looked up, she saw in front of her huge jagged boulders making her way impassable. As she looked to the left, further along the beach, she realised it was clear of any boulders. All she had to do was to walk a little way to the left and she could get back up quite easily. She felt this dream was telling her something very significant. It showed that she knew there were two ways of looking at her life and how she could act. She 'knew' of both the 'A' version of how it could be and the 'Z' one preventing it. The dream made her realise more deeply that 'knowing' this was not enough to enable her to let the 'Z' beliefs go.

WAYS OF MAINTAINING THE 'Z' PATTERNS OF FEELING, THINKING AND BEHAVING

One of the main ways people manage to maintain their belief that their particular 'Neurotic Solution' cannot be changed is by denying there is any other form of 'Attachment' either worth having or even available to them, other than the one they originally created in order to remain Attached to their original 'care givers'. An example of this was shown by a man who never allowed himself to experience any proper valuation of himself, in spite of the fact that he was exceptionally gifted. He was academically clever, had a high level of physical prowess, was good looking, did extremely well at work, was popular and had a lovely family. In spite of all these ways of feeling good about himself, apparently available to him, he blocked off feeling lovable, or that to openly or verbally express deep love for anyone, was barred from him. It took him a long time to recognise how his 'Z' pattern was keeping him in his original 'Neurotic Solution', which had taken the form of making himself feel 'small' and that he was not a threat to his original 'care givers'.

Another example is of a woman who had married one of her cousins. She had given birth to a daughter some years previously. When she found herself pregnant again, later in life than she had expected, she was very thrilled and happy when a baby boy was born. Sadly, he did not live more than a few months. Her sense of both grief and guilt were so strong that, as she explained to me, she could only relieve those feelings by making a very strong decision. This was never to do anything again that she would not have been able to do had he lived. She said she had decided that she must never 'gain' anything from his death. Her decision completely altered her lifestyle. She stayed in every evening as if she had a small baby to look after. She cut herself off from any social life and appeared to be totally engaged in this 'Neurotic Solution', as if she did not deserve anything else. After having sympathised with her in the loss of a deeply loved baby, I also acknowledged her feeling that in some way she felt responsible for it too. Then I quietly aired the suggestion that after such a severe loss, rather than punishing herself for it, perhaps she might find comfort from the pain she was in, by turning to her friends and doing things that she loved. It seemed she could not accept any such way of thinking and, as I only knew her through a friend, I was left wondering where this need to be 'punished' had originally come from.

THE SENSE OF HAVING TO 'PAY' FOR ANY 'A' EXPERIENCES

Unfortunately, another way of maintaining the notion that the 'Neurotic Solution' is the only safe way to exist is to go through another form of suffering, any time that an 'A' perception is thought about or actually experienced. There seem to be three ways in which to engage in this. The first is to bring in a level of expectation of something that someone would like to do, which challenges the 'Z' perception of how they 'have to be'. I have written about this as a 'before' method, which means the suffering is created in an endeavour to stop the person acting, or even believing in an 'A' way of being. An example of this is the woman who had diarrhoea prior to planning any journey away from home. The next way is, as someone clearly described it, 'mucking it up' at the time. For example, the woman who so wanted to feel happy when her grandsons were with her, but when they came she was so anxious she could not enjoy any of it. A very common version of experiencing the 'Z' version of thinking is the third form of 'paying' for it, I have described as 'after'. An example of this has already been given, where men achieve sex with their partners when they have an excessive fear of failure and immediately tell themselves that they will 'never be able to achieve it again'.

Sometimes this kind of sense of 'payment' enables people to see both how unrealistic their 'Z' ways of thinking really are, while at the same time respecting how and why they created them. It can sometimes be the start of a 'breakthrough'.

ANGER TOWARDS 'Z' FEELINGS

Some people have very angry feelings towards their pain and suffering and see it as somehow 'separate' from themselves to such an extent that they can rage against it. They tend to say such things as they want to 'kill it off', or they want to 'cut it out', as if in fantasy it could be surgically removed. When people feel this angry with their ways of thinking and feeling, I try hard to get them to look back again at the events that were occurring in their lives when they were very small. If they have already told me in detail about how they endured whatever their individual pain was, I generally asked them what they think was the reason why they had developed their specific ways of reacting. I urge them to think far more kindly towards themselves. Some people are able to see that they were always made to feel 'wrong' or 'bad', 'unwanted' or 'unacceptable'. These were the perceptions of themselves that they were given by their 'care givers'. They are then again in touch with the helpless feelings they had then and, in some way or another, manage to recognise that in the circumstances they felt that they had no alternative but to respond to their 'care giver's' views in whatever way they could.

Some of them will recognise that this is what they are still believing now and what is still determining so much of their current thinking and behaviour. I may then try again in different ways to ask them why they are just strengthening the view that they were given, that gives them so much pain, instead of striving in every possible way to discover how to find a different version of themselves: one that feels real, free of pain, and appropriate to who they are now. I suggest that part of this discovery does require them to think more kindly, sympathetically and even generously about how they coped at the time. This opens up the opportunity to suggest that they have grown up, believing this

version of themselves is true, when it is nothing of
again encourage the person to feel they need to reco
they really are.

ATTITUDE OF SOME 'CARE GIVERS'

I do believe that there are some 'care givers' who would be shocked and very upset if they realised how much distress they have actually caused the children they were looking after. I believe that for some of them this is because they are genuinely out of touch with their own Attachment histories. They may be unaware of attitudes they hold and the prejudices that they are acting out. They may be, as suggested in a previous section, just too tired, ill, or disorganised to give the child in their care the love and affection that every child needs in order to build up a proper valuation of themselves.

Dr. Alice Miller wrote much about the effects of care given to children in their early years. She held very strongly to the view that if a child has even one adult who shows both that they care about them and respect them and above all realise what the child is going through, this can give that child a better perception of themselves. I have certainly found that those adults who remember the part such a person played in their lives seem to be able to relate to others in a more positive way.

Dr. Miller told a fragment of a story to illustrate what she was writing about when parents seem oblivious of the effect that their behaviour is having on their children. She described two young parents who were with their small son, aged about two or three years old, in a park. The parents had just bought ice lollies on sticks. They were sucking them with enjoyment and laughing and teasing the boy when he begged for a lick of them. They pulled away, saying that he couldn't have any. He went on begging to have some, but their teasing and laughter and dodging away from him went on until they had finished their lollies. At this point the father offered his child the stick. He looked at it and threw it away in disgust and disappointment. The boy became upset, but the parents, still treating it as a big joke, walked on.

Dr. Miller is in no way making out that one small incident of this nature on its own is responsible for future serious emotional problems in the child. What she was trying to do was to use it as an illustration of how 'out of touch' many adults are with their own memories of how it feels as a small child to be treated as if 'they didn't matter', their feelings not only being ignored, but treated as a joke.

'NOBODY CAN BE AS "BAD" AS ME'

This remark is common among those in long-term therapy who struggle with the pain of their symptoms and express how equally 'hard' it is to try and change them. They express a fear that they are going to be the one who is 'incurable', their condition is so 'bad'. They air fears that the therapist will 'give up on them' for that reason. Hidden within this fear there also seems to be some kind of challenge to the therapist. It is as if part of the client is saying, 'you aren't any good, you won't be able to "cure me".' This kind of thinking is described by some analysts as a source of what they define as 'gratification'. In other words, the client is struggling to get a sense of being more 'powerful' than the therapist, making them agree that the client's 'Z' way of being cannot be changed by anyone.

I tend not to see it as a 'challenge', but openly acknowledge that therapists do not and indeed cannot 'cure' people. I suggest very mildly that this is a combined task and that all I can ever do is try and help people to discover ways to change for themselves. In this way, the changes become something that belong to them and cannot be taken away, nor are they the product of pills, or drink, or something outside themselves.

PROJECTION AND TRANSFERENCE

One of the ways 'Neurotic Solutions' are maintained into adult life is the projection on to other people of the same responses aroused by their early 'care givers'. Although this is something that we all do to a certain extent all the time, it is often the hardest one for the person concerned to recognise. For example, most of us tend to feel warmly towards someone who reminds us of some other person we once knew whom we liked, without necessarily recognising the 'connection' consciously. Similarly, the opposite occurs, so that we may find ourselves tending to dislike someone almost immediately on meeting because they too remind us of someone who once treated us badly or who looks like the sort of person we fear or disapprove of, without giving the new person time to show that they are in fact quite different! Our instant likes and dislikes are far less rational than we would like to believe!

Those who have had a 'Secure Attachment' will tend to expect a benign and generally friendly response from the people they meet. If this is not forthcoming, they will neither 'attack', nor 'run away'. They will make a measured appraisal of the situation and will generally act appropriately. They will not unduly expose themselves to danger, neither will they imagine personal hostility to be there if it is not.

If however the person has had an 'Insecure Attachment', depending on the severity of their experiences, they may be unaware of how deep their fears and anger are hidden within themselves. This may make them expect their managers, for example, to want to 'do them down' and respond to them in a variety of negative ways. Some may fear that they will 'never be accepted' and these people may try endlessly to please and placate their managers or anyone above them, just as they felt they had to with their early 'care givers'. Some may be so fearful of the power that they feel others hold over them that they will frequently change jobs, expecting it to 'always be like this'. In this way the person may continue to respond to others, just as he or she felt they always had to, in order to survive with their original 'care givers'. An example of this might be someone who expects people not to like them, and who could start psychotherapy anticipating that some form of rejection will inevitably be there and will start 'on the defensive' before it begins. When this way of behaving occurs in relation to the therapist, it is known as 'Transference'. This only means the person is transferring one way of feeling from one person to another, without realising it. Psychotherapists who specialise in working in this way describe it as 'transference' from their clients and 'Counter Transference' in relation to the therapist's response.

For therapists, recognition of this way that we all behave is of vital importance. Some therapists who would describe themselves as 'Kleinians' (having gone through a 'Kleinian' training) work very largely by understanding their clients' responses in this way, through their own responses to the way their clients behave. Many books have been written detailing at great length the way 'Transference' is used in psychotherapy.

I believe that it is important for all therapists to be very sensitive to any emotion that is expressed, but to be equally aware when there is an absence of an emotion that might be expected but which remains unspoken about. This can be due to so many reasons. The person may be consciously withholding feelings if they do not fully trust the therapist. This happens in ordinary relationships too. On other occasions the person in therapy may be holding back feelings associated with early memories, because they are too frightening to recognise, let alone speak about.

It is very easy to say that someone is 'in denial'. This is often said in a somewhat derogatory way, as if this is done consciously. It is more likely to be covering a deep fear of some event. One of the most common is when someone feels unable to face the death of someone very close to them, someone that the person feels they cannot bear to lose. They may not be able to admit such a loved person is ill, let alone face the thought of living without them. Some people manage the reality of the loss better than their imagined version. Others sadly often die within a year, according to Dr. Parkes who did a lot of research into mortality rates in widows.

Occasionally people in therapy will act out their feelings in the relationship with their therapist in a very direct way. In one centre that I worked in, a young woman arrived each time so drunk that she could not use the session. She had shared a good deal of her circumstances with me earlier. She was the younger of two girls with elderly parents. She saw herself as being 'born too late'. She felt that her parents had no time or energy for her. She felt this was in stark contrast to how they responded to her older sister. Each time she came to the centre I wondered how she had even got on the bus. I made her a black coffee and spread out three of the big cushions we always had available for groups. Within minutes she was asleep. If the room was not needed by anyone else, I generally left her there until shortly before I was due to leave. I would then wake her and she was generally more capable of getting herself off than she had been on her arrival. I always said that I was sorry that she had not felt capable of using the time available, but without expressing any recriminations. Her other behaviour that understandably annoyed my colleagues was the way she would telephone the centre and rage away in a voice blurred by alcohol, until she had filled the centre's answerphone. Soon after this she started to call me at my home, generally around 3am.

When the phone woke me, all I could ever hear was her heavy breathing. She made no attempt to talk. I knew it was her and suggested that, as she had woken me up, she might gain something from talking, but she just put the phone down. At this point, I decided to point out to her that by calling at that hour she was also waking up my husband and that this was neither a fair or kind thing to do. Soon after this she stopped calling my home.

Later, when I asked her what she thought she was gaining by calling me and not speaking, she gave a very coherent account. She said that she wanted me to understand the pain she felt and had experienced for so for many years of being ignored, treated as if she was a 'nobody' and not worth anything. She wanted to make sure that she 'stayed in my head'. When she told me this, I felt it made sense of all her behaviour. When I said that that was not the way I thought I had ever treated her, she agreed.

A few weeks after this, a crisis arose as she lost her job. The way she responded to that could have had very tragic consequences. Quite late one evening I received a call at home from her. She was drunk, but was able to tell me that she had spent the last of her Benefit money on a single train ticket to a rather remote seaside resort. She had bought six cans of beer which she had drunk and was on her own in a small bay. She then said she was going to swim out to sea until she could go no further. She was apparently intending to end her life in this way.

In the last few months she had spoken about her love of the sea and of a vague dream she had had about wanting to make her life in a seaside town. She was calling from a public telephone box that did not take calls back. I could only presume such a call box was there because it was such an isolated spot. She had obviously kept back enough of the right coins to call me, but inevitably the money ran out. She had finally rendered me incapable of doing anything to help her or to experience the same sense of total helplessness and being useless that she had described to me earlier, that she herself had felt for so long. I remember feeling so sad at the thought that, however hard one may try to 'be there' for someone differently from how they had experienced this from others before, there was no guarantee that she experienced it as strong enough to counter her determination to act out her 'Neurotic Solution'.

To my utter astonishment, a few moments later the phone rang again. This time it was the local telephone operator over two hundred miles away, who had overheard the call and wanted to know who I was. I told her that I was the person's therapist. She then asked if I would like her to call the police. I said, 'yes, as soon as possible', as I believed there was a real risk involved. I gave her my name and address and said that they could be given on to the police. About two hours later a call came from a police station from the nearest town to the beach. I was told first that they had arrested her on the basis that to do so was 'in her own interest'. She would spend a night in a police cell and, provided that I would guarantee paying for a train warrant for her to return to her home town, they would see that she got on a train in the morning.

Later I paid that sum into my local police station and marvelled at the caring police and telephonist in that distant seaside place. I was glad that I had been able to warmly thank them for acting so quickly and responsibly. Much to my surprise, she came to the centre at her usual time the following week, perfectly sober. It seemed that, on her return, she had gone to see her sister, who had helped her put her flat on the market. Later it seemed that it had sold very quickly, so she had gone down to the seaside town that she had always dreamed of living in, and had found a flat that was far cheaper than her present one. She told me that it would have far more space, where she could paint, which I knew was the one thing she loved doing. I hoped that this might help to keep her spirits up until she found work and settled in.

I inevitably spent time thinking about how such a seemingly rapid change could occur, in what had appeared a very entrenched 'Neurotic solution'. She corresponded with me, at her request, for a year or two and seemed calmer, telling me that she felt more 'at peace' than she had ever done before. She put it down to living by the sea making her feel happy. I could not help thinking that if it was that simple she might have organised it for herself some years earlier. What made a lot of sense to me was that she took a huge gamble on spending her last bit of money on calling me to confront me with being unable to act in a helpful or supportive way. It was as if she wanted to tell me that she knew her 'Neurotic Solution' (though of course they are not the words she would have used) would always be like that and that it could never be changed. She did not know then that the telephonist would act as she did, nor the police, who were apparently very kind to her, nor for sure that I would enable her to return home.

Other therapists may interpret the reasons for this outcome quite differently. I think it was because, at that point, she was able to believe there were people who treated her as a valued and worthwhile person and, against all odds, acted on this. I think that this enabled her to perceive herself in a different way and so to act differently from how she had done before. This type of rapid reversing of a 'Neurotic Solution' is most likely to happen when the person's real life situation is threatened by it in an important and very serious way. This may be the case even when the person themself is not fully aware of the reason why they feel able to act differently. The event has to be such that the loss involved in acting out their 'Neurotic Solution' feels more dangerous to their real life than giving it up. In this case it really was, possibly putting her life at risk. Sometimes it may be that the person realises that their marriage, or some other relationship that means a great deal to them, is seriously at risk if they continue to act out their 'Neurotic Solution'.

Another young woman, who had suffered the most severe long drawn-out sexual abuse that I had ever known, who often engaged in self harm, and who had made at least one suicide attempt, came to a session and told me that she had very recently engaged in some self-harm that could very seriously damage her. I again felt that I was in some sense being deeply challenged, as if I was being told 'nothing can be any different'. I do not know if I was in a particularly sensitive mood that day, but I was so shocked and I guess upset to think that someone so far into therapy could still do this to herself that I could not stop tears coming to my eyes. I quickly blinked them away, hoping that she had not seen them, as to show such feelings went against all my training, but I realised that she had. Did she too need to know that someone cared about her enough to respond to the pain she had inflicted on herself? What followed amazed me. Within a very short time, she took action in a completely new way. She left her abusive partner, filled her car with all her personal belongings and went back to her hometown. In due course she got a divorce, married again a very different man and had two children. She has kept in touch with me at her request and since then has coped with the most demanding situations imaginable within her family, in a way that very few people could do.

These kinds of responses make me understand what Bowlby actually means when he says that therapists only have any deep impact on their clients if they make a real relationship with them. Above all, he considered that therapists should strive to create what he calls a 'Secure Base'. I believe that, however hard we may try to do this, there are inevitably times when we fall short of both. But I think most clients feel it keenly if they experience their therapist trying to do this and succeeding most of the time.

REGULARISING

At this point, I want to describe a very basic concept of what lies at the core of good mental health. This in general is one shared by all the major theories, though inevitably it is expressed in very different words. It is to do with reconciling the most extreme conflict that exists in all humans. Some philosophers may see it as the factor that differentiates humans from animals. In brief, it is the conflict that arises from loving and hating the same person.

This conflict is seen by Freud as the need to reconcile the primitive, volatile 'Id' (as he called it) with the severe, restricting 'super- ego', by the eventual harmonising done through the 'ego'. Kleinians talk about harmonising the conflict between the 'good breast' and the 'bad breast' which comes through reaching the 'Depressed Position': language which again is difficult for many people to understand. Jungians describe finding a balance between the male and female aspect of the personality. Attachment Theorists use the word 'regularising' as the way to resolve these extreme emotional conflicts. All these theories recognise the three parts of the mind.

Alice Miller's story told earlier of the father who refused and teased his small son when he pleaded to have a share of his ice lolly, and failed to help his child feel an included, loved and safe member of his family. By offering the boy the lolly stick, in contrast to each of his parents having a whole lolly to themselves, he diminished the child's sense of value. Such an incident leaves a child struggling with feelings of wanting their parents' love, but feeling an acute sense of being rejected. Such an incident is of course a 'drop in the bucket', but 'drop by drop' is the way our sense of an 'insecure self' comes about. The sense of feeling a 'secure sense of self' also comes from a gradual process, as we slowly become confident that we are not likely to be overcome by extreme emotions that will defeat us.

For many parents, one of the dreaded moments comes when their two year old throws what is commonly called a 'temper tantrum' in a public place, such as a supermarket. The immediate sensation for most parents is that everyone can hear the screaming and yelling and will be highly critical of their child's behaviour. In the past, and sometimes now, a hauling up of the child and a big wallop with loud scolding would be the outcome, or an angry disowning of the child and the parent moving away. Both these responses, so understandable, come from the idea that the child is 'spoilt', 'naughty', 'wants their own way'. All are seen as 'bad'. Very few people understand that the child is fearful, overcome by their emotions and feeing unable to handle them at this stage of life.

If the parent can concentrate on their child and overcome the sense of criticism emanating from other people in the store, they can appreciate that their child is struggling to deal with feelings of anger and fear at being thwarted. (These are, after all, feelings that we all know about ourselves.) If the parent can then stay calm and quiet beside their child and, in a little while, suggest that he or she will feel better soon and, if they stop yelling, that they could come with her, as she has to get something for tea and they could help choose a favourite pudding, cake or whatever. This is not the place to move away, gently, as it might be at home, giving the child time to recover, but calm behaviour by the parent with an ordinary insistence that 'life has to go on,' without rushing, generally leads to the child getting up, still gulping and tearful, but feeling 'all is not lost'. They have felt 'stayed with' not deserted or made to feel 'bad'. This is not 'bribery' or 'giving in', as so many people might condemn it, instead it is offering the child a small sense of control over the proceedings, to feel 'understood' and not so alone. A hug and an encouraging smile helps the child regain their 'sense of self'. He or she is on the long road of learning to 'regularise' their feelings.

In Section Four that follows, I attempt to write more about the ways most people who struggle with long term 'Neurotic Solutions' can work their way out of these patterns of feelings and behaviour and secure better feelings about themselves.

SECTION FOUR

PAINFUL LIFE-LONG PATTERNS CAN CHANGE.

In this section, I want to set out what I believe needs to be worked on by the individual concerned in order to achieve sufficient freedom from the emotional disturbances that have caused them long-term suffering. Setting out and attempting to summarise this will inevitably mean re-capping some of the ways already described. I want not only to clarify them, but also to present them more chronologically.

MANY YEARS OF WORKING AS AN ATTACHMENT THERAPIST

It may appear arrogant that I am setting out my view that these lifelong patterns of feeling and behaving can be changed, in spite of all the types of resistance to doing so by those suffering from them that have already been described in previous sections. I can only do this because, over so many years of working as an Attachment therapist in a number of very different settings, I have worked with many people who have achieved it. Some have not managed to feel completely safe from their old ways of thinking and behaving all of the time, but they manage these in new ways that they feel they could not have done before.

The old patterns may strive very occasionally to haunt them again. By recognising them for what they are, they are no longer experienced as overwhelming. Far more often such people have said to me they can hardly believe the things they feel able to do now, which previously would have felt impossible.

ACKNOWLEDGING WORK THAT NEEDS TO BE DONE

I believe that real change in anyone's view of themselves (if they come into the group of people already defined) requires first of all for them to recognise fully that they are struggling with a severe conflict inside themselves. This recognition of both sides of the conflict needs to be talked about openly and fully. This is probably best done with a psychotherapist or experienced councillor. As well as this, the person concerned needs to appreciate the depth of their feelings attached to both sides. The reasons for these depths need to make sense to them too. This is no trivial matter. It may be achieved by some relatively quickly, for others it may take some years.

To achieve this recognition of the conflict and to talk openly and freely about it, and slowly to understand how their particular pattern of thinking, feeling and behaviour came about, needs time. I believe this is because the person concerned needs to feel that their therapist has properly and fully heard (not just listened) to the accounts of their clients' lives. However jumbled or distressing the person's stories may be, they often need to tell them many times before they can believe that they will not be judged, criticised or 'corrected' in any way. The therapist needs to give recognition to the courage required to do this, as visiting all the old memories can be very distressing, as can talking about current pain. Gradually, as the person feels able to tell their story and feels assured that it will be believed, they start to realise how they came to adapt their perception of themselves in order to find a way to survive in the home of their original 'care givers'. This may have been their own home in which they were born, or those of others who were 'parenting' them. Above all, they recognise there was at the time a strong drive within them to survive, which forced them to find a 'solution'. It may have been to 'bow to', or 'accept' the version of themselves that was on offer. Others may have learned to 'keep a low profile', or to 'hide' or to 'fight'. There are as many different ways of discovering a 'solution' to this absolute need to 'survive' as the number of people who struggle to find it. This is because each version of 'the concept of themselves' is unique.

When someone reaches this stage of understanding for themselves how they have built up their personal and painful perception of themselves, they seem more able to at least see that a different way of feeling about themselves might exist.

They need to recognise that the 'other side' of themselves, that does not want to go on experiencing endless-seeming pain and grief, has a strong force within them too! This is the part of them that longs to find a sense of security, but they need to realise that **it has to be found in a different way, and not through the 'Neurotic Solution'.**

I believe that it is very important for people who are caught up in this type of conflict to believe that they are 'good' people, not 'bad' or 'wrong', as so many of them seem to feel. They need help in recognising that this sense of feeling so undervalued is a distorted view, but it was the only one available to them at the time. I sometimes describe this experience as something they felt 'obliged to buy', at the time. It is important to help people change the image that they have of themselves. I am not suggesting for one moment engaging in false praise, but I encourage them to recognise the courage and resourcefulness in themselves, often at an early age, that led them to find a 'solution' to their sense of feeling so insecure. For so many, it has meant learning to live with their own specific sense of feeling deeply devalued.

To many people who have had a 'Secure Attachment', it may be hard even to imagine how it feels for people who have had very 'Insecure Attachments'. Everyone needs to realise that the way such people cling to their suffering, and maintain it in various ways as well, are not 'feeble' or 'stupid'. Even more important to establish is the concept that for such people to change their suffering feelings, or to 'let them go' is felt, to varying degrees, 'terrifying' for the person concerned. To begin with, as already described, it can feel impossible to do. I am afraid very few people understand how, let alone why, those people long to be free of their suffering, and yet feel so incapable of change.

The conflict at first can seems so 'one sided'. The 'Z' version feels so vastly stronger than the 'A' one. The work involved in this change generally comes gradually. Freedom from it needs to be experienced as a 'right', as a 'given', never having to be 'paid for'. It comes eventually from a strong recognition that **the person is no longer in the situation of feeling a helpless child**. Now there is not such a limited source of people around them as there was in their early lives. In their young lives so many people have felt that they were a burden to their 'care givers', unwanted, a nuisance, someone who caused them pain. Some have grown up feeling themselves a 'terrible trouble', carrying an impossible task of meeting the emotional, physical or sexual needs of their 'care givers'. As already described, one of the most damaging perceptions of the self occurs when children feel their 'care givers' treat them as though they did not exist.

The recovery out of all these very varied perceptions of themselves requires the person concerned to fully recognise all the complicated manoeuvres that they are engaged in, through their feelings and thoughts and behaviour, that have **maintained** these early perceptions of themselves. Again and again they need to see that these perceptions had to be 'bought', only in order to remain Attached, as this provided a version of security needed for their sense of survival. They have to go on to see that it was a 'solution' **only of use to them in their original early environment.** It is no 'solution' now in their present life. In fact it is their very inappropriateness that causes their present suffering.

Gradually, not only is its inappropriateness recognised, but its utter futility is seen too. The person needs to realise that what they are doing is continuing to believe in and to act out the very same damning version of themselves in the present that they were given in the past. The hardest part for them to talk about is the concept that they are making a 'choice' to stay with their suffering. I try not to use the word 'choice' because I fully recognise how unreal that feels to them. It only makes sense when they understand how and why 'letting go' of their suffering feels so scary, so it never feels like a simple 'choice' to them.

There are some situations when a person describes an awareness of an irksome habit, that may well be relatively easily changed by a conscious decision to do so. But I am referring to people who have a long-term struggle with very painful and stressful feelings about themselves, that often lead them to behave in quite cruel ways towards themselves and sometimes towards others too. These generally do take a long time to change. To talk as if it were simple for such people to change would show a complete lack of knowledge about how our minds work.

THE BELIEF THAT 'Z' WAYS OF THINKING ARE 'UNCHANGEABLE'

It is very important to emphasise that the people that persist in experiencing their 'Z' perception of themselves as 'impossible to change' recognise the reasons for holding this view. It lies at the heart of 'Z' ways of thinking, feeling and behaving, as they are perceived when originally formed as the **only way** of staying safely Attached to the particular environment the person is in. This pattern of belief is then set to be continued **at all costs**, however distressing it may be to endure. It comes to be accepted by the person concerned, as 'their lot', defining their sense of self in the process.

There are two main ways that such people maintain their belief that to 'suffer' is the only way they can be. The first is to put themselves again and again into situations that repeat their early experiences. For example, they will relate to someone in such a way that they will get hurt or rejected and then feel abandoned all over again. The second way is to fail to recognise that a better and more realistic perception of themselves is available. For example, they may be doing well at work, or have achieved success in other parts of their lives; there may even be a relationship that is safe to be had, but they will feel unable to see it in that way. All of these will be totally discounted, because of the continued drive to hold on to an 'unworthy' or very distressing sense of themselves.

The hard part for such people to recognise is how these ways of feeling and behaving have largely been occurring **out of their conscious awareness**.

THE THIRD PART OF MIND COMES TO OUR RESCUE

Gradually over time, the third part of mind gets stronger. It is no longer perceived as the 'Helpless Observer' of the conflict between 'A' and 'Z'. It becomes experienced as a part of the person's thinking at a conscious level, that can intervene through understanding the ways that the conflict between 'A' and 'Z' affects their perception of themselves. It is through this 'third' part that the person is enabled to recognise that their current sense of security is no longer dependent on 'Z' ways of perceiving themselves. Instead, the person needs to move to the reality of 'A' thinking. This provides a sense of feeling calm, being in control of themselves, and above all feeling a sense of contentment. The person then becomes aware that the belief that the 'A' way of being is 'too risky', has to be 'paid for', or, at worst, is 'impossible to change', is the **'Z's' perception of 'A''** in an attempt to once again impose the belief that the 'Z' way is the only one.

It is the third part of mind that eventually helps the person to see that the 'Z' way of thinking about themselves is no longer needed or appropriate as a way of feeling secure in their adult life. They slowly come to realise that the need for a sense of security that is found through their sense of self can never be found through the 'Z' way. Bit by bit they do see the unreality of the 'Z' perception. As the person discovers their 'A' way of feeling does exist, so their fear of letting go their 'Z' ways disappears.

'KNOWING' IS NOT ENOUGH

Some people know only too well about their conflict. They may experience short periods of feeling free of their 'Z' patterns and then despair as they plunge back in again, experiencing the sense of 'punishing' themselves for having tasted 'A' once more. Understanding and knowing all the 'inside out' of 'how' and 'why' this may be still may not always be enough to enable them to feel reliably free of their 'Z' patterns in a more long-term stable way.

A DEEP WISH TO CHANGE

From some deep level of the person's sense of self has to come **a real wish to change**. This is not easy to talk or even write about, as some people may ardently say 'but I do want to change more than anything else'. This point is probably the pivotal one, as the person comes to fully recognise the fear involved in changing a pattern of feeling and thinking about themselves that they have had for a very long time.

Some years ago, the psychologist Dorothy Rowe wrote of one of her 'patients', describing this moment as like ' jumping out of an aeroplane without a parachute'. That action carries certain death! I think, although it may be an attempt to describe the depth of fear involved, this perception needs to be seen as unreal as the person's 'Z' concept of 'A'. It is a false picture to sustain the notion that to give up 'Z' threatens their survival. In fact, at this stage the very opposite is the truth, for when the 'A' place is experienced fully, it holds all that the person wants in the way of feeling calm, in control and with a sense of security that comes from finding a proper 'sense of self'. As one person wrote, 'days are good and real for me now, I never want to leave this place because I know this is real and where I should always have been'.

THREE STEPS TO BE TAKEN

I believe that there are three further steps that have to be taken. For many people, these may have to be taken again and again, as the person struggles to be free of their old pattern of thinking and behaving.

The first is TO RECOGNISE 'Z' thinking, feeling and behaviour. That means the person 'being on guard', being their own detective, or monitor, or any description that fits the individual person's way of recognising an awareness of a 'Z' type of thought, feeling or behaviour that they are immediately engaged in. For some people this level of self-awareness comes almost naturally. For others, such a level of constant awareness of their own thinking and feelings and a sharpened ability to 'see what they are up to' is painfully strange. They can easily 'write it off' as 'self-indulgence' or 'boring'. If these sorts of thoughts come, they in turn need to be 'seen through' straightaway as ones produced by 'Z' thinking, in order to maintain its 'hold'. Instead, the person needs to see intellectually and **feel at an emotional level** just how the 'Z' pattern has worked for them, to maintain itself. At this point they need to try and bring up the third part of their mind, 'the observer', which may be saying to them something like, 'you know you created the 'Z' way of feeling long ago, to try and make you feel secure, but now you know more than you did then'. If the person is able to manage this type of listening to themselves, they may then be able and willing to ask themselves, 'so where is this idea of being 'indulgent' or 'bored' coming from?' If they are capable of questioning themselves like this, they would know the source is 'Z' thinking. I believe that when someone realises that they have recognised in a new way a bit of 'Z' thinking, combined with the deep wish to be free of it, they are able to move to the second step.

This is TO REJECT 'Z' thinking. If this can be done **at once**, at the time, it starts to affirm the person's belief that they, not someone else, or something else, can change them. If in a therapy session such a situation arises, the person's 'Z' way of thinking will often try every possible way to regain control. If that person feels able to trust me and tells me out loud what they are genuinely thinking, they may well say something like, 'I can't hear the 'A' voice. I can't stop the 'Z' one, it is too strong.' The way I try and help the person deal with these 'moments', is to suggest that they see the 'Z' ones as occurring just at that moment! That really is all they are! There is no need to think in terms of trying to change their whole life in one 'go' now! It is just swift thinking that is needed in order to respond to recognising a 'Z' thought and then moving on to reject it, ***just on this occasion***. This actually takes less time than it does to write this description of such an event.

Far more often, I will listen to an account shared in a more leisurely way. It would go something like this: 'Last week I was invited to go somewhere, or perhaps to do something, I wanted to say yes, but I was just about to say no, and invent an excuse, something I have done before hundreds of times. I spotted it as the old 'Z' way of behaving and then I suddenly said 'yes' instead. It was odd, as I almost felt surprised, as if someone else was saying it!' The person then went on to describe how immediately afterwards she found herself needing to think she could always ring up later and say she couldn't go and not do it after all. I then asked her if she had 'spotted' that, as another 'Z' intervention, to try and make her feel that what she had done was too 'risky'. This opened up a much bigger recognition. She spoke about how, thinking that she could 'get out of' doing something she would previously have felt too scared to do, the 'Z' voice had seemed at first rather 'comforting'. Then it became stronger, until all the old fears crept in, as she had thoughts that she would 'make a mess of it', feel 'stupid' or 'embarrassed', or even 'panic' if she did go. She then said somehow seeing where these ideas had come from, she was all the more determined to go, and then said, although it was 'very hard getting there', she had gone, it was a success and she actually enjoyed it. With marvellous honesty, she then admitted she hadn't really wanted to tell me that. When I asked her if she knew the reason why, she felt that she was again able to be open up about it and said she feared I would think she was 'all right' now and therapy would be ended. We were both able to laugh a bit over this, as I said that I had no such thoughts, as she would end her therapy when she was ready. Meanwhile I was glad she had a glimpse of an 'A' feeling and got a real idea of how to find it. Above all, she had recognised the 'before' way of her 'Z' thinking, which made absolute sense to her.

The third step is TO ACT. Taking action is as important as the other two previous steps. This again only applies to that moment of recognition and rejection of a 'Z' thought or feeling as it appears. The main part of this process is to act immediately. It means quickly moving, or doing something else. It does not matter much what it is, but most helpfully something small that needs doing. This takes the person's mind on to something else and they are distracted from the 'Z' way of thinking. The really important point of it all is that the person is engaged in all three processes. They are engaged with conscious understanding of the role of all three steps. As a result, most people who have this kind of experience gain some sense of being more in control of themselves. Whether they have made a phone call, sent an email, decided to drive down a new route, or simply done something like tidying up papers, or done the washing, it is as a chosen new act. They have responded differently. They have not allowed the old 'Z' pattern to continue to dominate, to rush in, with another version. Even if that happens a bit later, the person is in a new state of awareness. They have made a small shift in the perception of themselves as someone who can determine who or how they want to be.

I am not underestimating for one moment the mammoth task it is for some people to make a long-lasting change in their 'sense of self', but if making a real change can be seen as *not* something that has all to be done *today*, as this can then so readily be seen as 'far too big a mountain' to climb. If change can be seen instead as something to recognise, reject and then to act differently towards, just at moments, then some notion of how it might really happen begins to emerge that feels less terrifying, or impossible. Above all, the person has experienced not having to obey the 'Z' voice has not led to anything dreadful happening. Even if only for a few moments, they have had a sense of feeling 'different', calmer and more in charge of themselves and being how they deep down want to be, feeling secure in themselves.

FINAL SUMMARY OF 'NEUROTIC SOLUTIONS'

For those readers who may still be uncertain about the meaning of 'Neurotic Solutions', I will attempt a final summary of their characteristics. Everybody to varying degrees has their 'sense of self' largely determined by the kind of 'Attachment' experience they have had during the early part of their lives, whoever their early 'care givers' happened to be.

This book has concentrated on those people who have had a variety of 'Insecure Attachments' at the early stage of their lives.

This has led them to having, in some cases, severe emotional distress which comes from their 'sense of self', leading to them suffering in a highly individual way, as already described. **The essence of this form of suffering is that the person concerned is as distressed by enduring their symptoms as they are at the thought of giving them up**. This is due to each person having to 'fit in' with whatever view of themselves they could get as they strove for a 'sense of security' with whatever the situation their original 'family' demanded, in order for them to stay 'Attached'. **This is the origin of the 'Neurotic Solution'**. The need to fully understand it has also to include the major ways in which each individual maintains this 'sense of self', however much distress it may give them. For many people it can last for the whole of their lives, unless there are certain interventions which enable changes to occur.

There are two main ways that 'Neurotic Solutions' are then maintained. The first is to support the belief that the way the person feels about themselves and the suffering that they endure cannot be changed because there is **'no other way of feeling or being'**. To give it up feels like having 'nothing', or being 'nothing', with no concept of how they might be if free of their painful sense of being 'wrong' or 'bad', or inadequate in some fearful way.

I believe this is the most important concept to be understood, as it tends to determine an enormous amount of the way such people conduct their lives. They all hold hard onto the belief that there are no other good ' Attachment' experiences available to them. Often they feel unable even to see them, let alone move towards them. This leaves them open to the enormous strength of their primary instinctive drive, to continue to perceive themselves as they felt forced to do so originally, **however inappropriate it may be to continue to do so in their adult lives.**

Such a belief is also one that is very difficult for many people without this type of patterning to comprehend. This belief that 'there is no other way of being' can be the source of their deepest distress, leaving them feeling trapped in an unendurable way.

The second main way the 'Neurotic Solution' is maintained is for the person to feel they have to 'pay' by suffering even more if they dare to move into feeling free of their suffering pattern. I have already described the three ways with examples of how this form of resistance to change can occur. It may be '**before**' the person plans to behave or feel differently. This takes the form of acute anxiety about doing so. This may come during a time when the person has dared to think about, or maybe anticipated, a possible time of being in a 'non-suffering' place, full of potential for happiness, or a sense of enjoyment, feeling calm or in control of themselves. This can then be dismissed as impossible, or can even fail to be recognised at all. The second way occurs '**during**' a time of change, already quoted as 'being mucked up' so that all the good feelings disappear. The third way of 'paying' for daring to change and emphasising how 'risky it can be' takes the form of suffering worse than ever '**after**' a time of change, however long or short it may be. I have previously described this in terms of a 'backlash' rather than a 'relapse' which feels so disheartening. It can at best lead to deeper understanding of why a person found changing in a particular way to be so threatening to their distorted 'sense of self'.

RESEARCH INTO PSYCHOTHERAPY

One of the most interesting findings from some research on psychotherapy is that, whatever theoretical framework the experienced therapist offers, generally something helpful and positive emerges. This is considered to be due to the main common factor in all therapies. It gives the person someone with the ability to offer their clients something that many of them may never have had before. This is a feeling of having their story fully heard and empathised with, in a real and proper way.

NO MIRACLE ANSWER

I believe there is no 'miracle answer' or 'cure' because eventually each person has finally to become their own therapist. They need to become gradually confident that, however hard their struggle to change has been, they have found a way of recognising their own painful patterns of thinking and behaving. I believe above all that they need to understand its source in a way that makes sense to them. In this way, they have come to see how and why it has dominated so much of their lives. What matters is that this process will help them to feel calmer, stronger and more in control of themselves. This comes from a proper evaluation of their 'sense of self'. It is this that gives them a realistic sense of security, which they feel belongs to them. It cannot be taken away by anyone or anything. To sum up once more, the person can relate to the quote already made: 'This is real and where I should always have been.'

SECTION FIVE

This section consists of different people's responses to this booklet. I asked for honest reactions to the information in it and the effect that it had on them. Some were already familiar with Attachment Theory, some were not. They come from very different backgrounds with a variety of life experiences.

RESPONSES

Judy Tweddle, a retired teacher, wrote: 'What a wonderful journey this booklet has taken me on and one I ended up feeling uplifted by and in a place of smiling recognition and newness at the same time, like watching a sunset or more appropriately a new dawn. A truly life-enhancing, life-affirming read.

The specifics that impacted on me the most were firstly how and why we use 'Neurotic Solutions' and this leading to the concept of 'Z' thinking.

Secondly, I felt as if I smiled out loud at the quotation about power, not over 'but the kind of power that enables others to develop and feel more confident about themselves'. This impacted on me in a very direct and specific way, as I shall explain later and helped me to recognise one of my own 'Neurotic Solutions.' I loved the clarity and power of the difference between 'like to be' and 'driven to be' and the awareness of this and the role of 'A' thinking.

Perhaps the best way, as I mentioned above, to endorse how I feel about this writing is to show how it immediately impacted on my personal situation and behaviour. Without becoming too detailed or indiscrete, I have a young male lodger whose circumstances have changed since he moved in, and I was concerned about this for my own sake.

Yesterday evening, before I had read Part Four, I happened to listen to a radio programme about suicide, and a Liverpool project to take on this enormous problem, particularly with young men. When I went to bed I was very aware of my lodger alone in his room and wondered about how he was feeling. It was a relief when I heard him go down to the kitchen. What I recognised in myself was my 'Avoidance Pattern' – being wary in an antipathetic way – of needy people, and their ability to invade my private space. This of course is my own fear of being needy and of having experienced feeling needy in a way that I had decided was 'weak'.

The effect of reading Part Four was to help me through this, as if it was my own personal therapy! I have a sense of myself as both a generous and extremely selfish person. Even now I am noticing where my 'Z' thinking has put the 'extremely'! The sense of duality is familiar, and the reading helped me see how relevant this is. I also connected very strongly with the notion of 'acting' and how that changes the internal and external dynamics. Doing something positive has often made me feel better, not only about myself but about the world.

It is now morning and I am happy that I have recognised the unhelpfulness of my wariness around my lodger, and to have seen that it has nothing to do with him. He is a strong, positive, cheerful young man, who has just emptied the drier and left my clean clothes out for me. He is also a vulnerable and lone young man, and I shall suggest we have supper together soon and catch up on how he is doing.

In this I recognise a feeling of relief, of lightness, of freedom from and therefore freedom to... a new dawn!'

Celia, a pattern cutter/theatrical costume maker, wrote: 'I really enjoyed reading this Paper as it gives a real insight into how and why we feel the way we do. Most books on this subject are written by academics only for their peers and the language used is hard to comprehend by most people not in the profession. This piece, with such understanding of what makes us who we are, will not only be a valuable addition for the author's colleagues, but for the average person with no experience of therapy will find this enlightening and a truly helpful way to understand why we react in the ways we do to some situations or events in our lives which can cause such distress.

I thought that the inclusion of the author's own experiences make you feel you are in contact with a real person who has a real comprehension of the subject she writes about.

I hope this will find its way into all libraries so that it will be of great help to all of us who try to find answers to our own emotional struggles.'

Katharine W., a G.P. currently working in an NHS urban practice, texted: 'A very large percentage of the patients who come to see me in the surgery have mental health problems. It is very difficult to get any kind of rapid psychiatric referral for them. I think this Writing should be available to psychiatrists, psychologists and other psychotherapists in the hope that more psychotherapists will be trained in the future.'

C. O., a care manager of both large and small retirement homes, wrote: 'I think this is a very clear and easy-to-read and follow document, in the understanding of how 'Neurotic Solutions' work in therapeutic practice. It is not overloaded with other references and readings. By carefully and sensitively unravelling behaviour, belief and thought, by building up the 'A' and safer place, it explains how this is achieved by working with the client at their pace and entering the place they are presenting either historically or currently.

It provides a deeper understanding of the therapist's position in the recognition of the client's need to feel that the therapist is also able to feel their pain. The client needs to feel this, in order to be fully engaged in the place that is real to the therapist. I don't see this as a challenge to the therapist, but for the client to ask the most difficult invitation for the therapist to come into a place of fear, uncertainty and darkness with them.

It helps that some personal experiences were included, as they clearly show the importance of the relationship of therapist/ client and how, although Attachment to the therapist is important in some cases, the author maintains strongly that the key aspect is for the client to form an Attachment to the whole okay person that they are striving to be.

The breaking down of barriers and pre-set beliefs is only possible to achieve when the person is at the point of not being overwhelmed by fear or behaviour, as in the marked improvement of women who had psychotherapy for psychosomatic vaginitis. This process is explained very clearly.

There is no way anyone can identify any individual client throughout the writing, other than that of the author and her brothers.

With her vast expanse of knowledge and experience the author manages to cover a huge range of therapeutic examples in the use of Person Centred Therapy.

Reading this as a 'client', I have really understood what the author is aiming to achieve.

Reading this as a 'professional' with some mental health experience and study, I would find this really helpful, particularly as a student.

I fully agree that Attachment Theory explaining that young children's experiences is the key to understanding the way we later develop and view life. I had many thoughts about my mother's early life, but on all the time I have worked on the abuse from my father, I have not understood or fully recognised how his life made him become an abuser. Maybe for me this is my next journey. This Writing has made me think more of that aspect and made me more determined to go on with my own writing.'

Chloe White, documentary film maker for 'Whalebone Films', wrote: 'The author asked me to read this book, as I have been working on a film that touches on similar issues. The film explores how a focus on Attachment Theory can help women in impoverished areas. The documentary is called *1001 Days* and focuses on a charity in South Africa called *Ububele*. The charity is based outside of Alexandra, a township near Johannesburg. Here, one of their projects is that they train local mothers to support other new mothers during the early days of their child's life. The theory being that the first 1001 days are the most important and can impact on everything from relationships to education, to careers, to mental health. The counsellors are taught certain sensitive parenting techniques that they can pass on to these mothers. The reason *Ububele* operate in this area is because Alexandra is poor and overcrowded and mothers raising families there report that they find their living conditions highly stressful. They describe experiencing their environment as pervasively dangerous and threatening. Their community is plagued by 70% unemployment, poverty and HIV. New mums often live alone, neglected by the father of the baby and thousands of miles from their extended families. 80% of the mums the home visitors meet had unplanned pregnancies and 73% report physical or emotional abuse. Although in many countries the importance of maternal and infant mental health and parent infant relationships is gaining increasing recognition, in South Africa it remains low on the political agenda. The pioneering women from this project are fighting this and believe that promoting resilience in infants and children is the best way to heal their community, particularly when the state has failed to deliver on the promises made after the fall of apartheid.

Pregnancy, birth and the first twenty-four months can be tough for every mother. For women living in Alexandra the appalling circumstances make it harder. But as the author highlights in her writing, it's during the early years that the foundations of a baby's mind are being put in place. Early events and relationships can affect the brain in ways that have lifelong consequences. Love and nurture from a caring adult teaches the baby to believe that the world is a good place and reduces the risk of them facing disruptive issues in later life. But when a mother is suffering stress or when a baby is exposed to maltreatment or domestic abuse, this can pass on the message that the world is dangerous. Children who don't receive loving, sensitive care are more likely to do worse in education, are less healthy and earn less, making it more likely that the cycle of harm is perpetuated in the following generation.

That's why the home visitors are so important. They are there, right at the very beginning, empowering new mothers to develop positive relationships with their babies at one of the most important times in a human being's life. Having received very little help from the government, these women know it is up to them alone to try to break the cycle of poverty and abuse in their beloved community, preventing problems before they arise and giving children the opportunity to lead healthy and fulfilling lives.'

<u>Judith Farrar, retired counsellor and current tutor</u>, wrote: 'It was a joy to read this paper and re-visit some of the amazing work of John Bowlby and the way Joan Woodward engaged us in it, when detachment seems the order of the day, with ever increasing mental health problems and fewer resources. This

paper reminds us of what is important to us as human beings and what is needed to help those who are suffering in so many ways.

My response isn't an academic one, more from someone who has been and in many ways still is involved in grass root mental health work as a social worker, counsellor and now in retirement an adult ed. tutor. The expansion of the theoretical ideas underpinning the practical application were welcome and especially enlightening.

Looking more deeply into why old patterns are so difficult to change is something that has interested me for a long time. I feel very privileged to have discussed this issue with the author in relation to individual people I have worked with over many years. The process of change and what makes it so complex seems to be at the heart of all the work. Believing that we all want to feel better leads to the questions around why this often doesn't happen, or takes so long and so much to make it happen. If only this question was at the heart of all mental health deliberations and concerns for the 'patient' rather than diagnosing someone with a pointless label! I remember hearing the author saying that for many clients the important issue was, 'How can I show the world what I have suffered, if I feel ok?' That sentence has always been in my considerations about what is happening to someone who feels so stuck in their old ways. The acknowledgement of suffering is so vital to the therapeutic process and I continue to hear stories of how people who have had a great deal of emotional suffering are treated like either naughty children for upsetting other people, or given more medication and labels to shut them up. It is one of my regular 'rants', I know, but I can never understand why the mental health services are so heavily populated with professional people devoid of compassion and even in a basic interest in helping someone feel better! It's almost like they become more and more contaminated the nearer they are to psychiatry and lose their humanity. I can't help feeling that this is a subject that would also make some interesting research if it hasn't been done already.

The most significant example of someone who could not give up her extremely serious self-harm responses/patterns was a young woman who had been seriously abused physically and emotionally by her mother. This had resulted in many hospital admissions. Her only response to extreme emotional pain was always to harm herself through cutting or burning, often putting her life at risk in the process. She was a very talented artist and the day centre where I worked held an art exhibition that was open to the public and family and friends of the artists. T's mother attended the exhibition and was heard to say to her daughter when viewing her work, 'There you are, I told you that you could do anything you wanted to do, if you made an effort.' No recognition about the reasons why her daughter had been unable to fulfil her potential and no responsibility for her part in reducing her daughter to becoming a long-term mental patient. The result was that T set fire to herself that evening, suffering severe burns, and this led to the start of her being moved to a long-term secure unit as an incurable case.

Tolerating the 'A' position and the 'backlash' are very useful ways to look at what is happening emotionally to someone who is struggling to break free from out-dated destructive patterns. Without these explanations, I think there is little hope of anyone understanding why such things happen. Tolerating feeling 'better' is a strange concept if it is void of any knowledge of the psychological process of change, or what might bring about the conflicts that arise because of it.

Through my community drama work I am still in touch with a number of people who have had long-term mental health problems. Some are valiantly trying to change their lives without any help these days, while others have 'good phases', then, when something triggers off old wounds, fall into the pit of despair. One such person, who only sees her psychiatrist for her to be used as a 'guinea pig' for the psychiatrist's new teaching post (not my assumption but straight from the psychiatrist's mouth), has been a 'self-harmer' all through her adult life and labelled everything from 'personality disordered', to 'borderline personality' to 'depressive' to 'schizophrenic'. She taught me more than anyone why people self-harm, ie in order to take away unbearable emotional pain, inflict physical pain, because it is easier to cope with and changes the focus.

In recent years she has been able to attend Worcester University and has a Foundation Degree. She has also held a family together as a single mother with no help at all. Both her children are high achievers and seem to be reasonably secure individuals, although I don't doubt they have been affected by their mother's difficulties. Her achievements have been totally ignored by the mental health professionals she has been in touch with. The psychiatrist, who is one of the better ones in this area, openly tells her she is 'personality disordered' and that she uses her in her teaching practice because she has all the diagnosable symptoms! This is a fact that isn't true at all, even if one were to subscribe to such a diagnosis. Even more importantly than failing to recognise her achievements, the psychiatrist fails to help her to understand and deal differently with her self- harming behaviour.

When I was her social worker, I remember sitting with her through such an episode in a day centre. For hours I tried to dissuade her from self-harm and to talk through what was happening instead. At the stage she was at it wasn't a good idea, as her compulsion to self-harm was so great, she went ahead with it anyway. I felt quite inadequate at the time and that it was beyond my expertise to help her, which I think was true. However the sad fact was, and still is, that psychiatry has nothing constructive to offer her either. In recent times I have advised her to be in touch with The Self-Harm Centre in Bristol, who continue to lead the way with advice to people who self-harm and provide training for mental health workers.

I enjoyed reading more about different kinds of 'Attachment'. Expansion on this is really helpful, especially for those with limited knowledge of Bowlby's work. Over the years I have begun to see the importance of Attachment in so many ways, for myself as well as others, in work environments as well as in personal relationships. Recognising the breaking of these, especially the forced breaking, is so necessary to understand the depth of despair and anxiety that can bring.

Considering the depth of suffering from the 'Neurotic Solution' is the only time I think I have understood what actually happens, when one is stuck in repeating the same pattern and why they are experienced as so essential to a sense of identity and safety. It really is so difficult 'letting go' of these patterns, as the author explains so well, is because they do hold at such depth and for so long our sense of identity and security. Staying with people through the resistance to change is not always understood, so to read it in black and white is both illuminating and encouraging.

There is a very helpful clear assessment built into all these sections, which I think encourages the 'client' to be able to see the cause and effect of their current situation. It goes far beyond merely identifying past experiences as causes of current distress, something I think happens all too often. It is as if locating the problem automatically solves it, rather than acts as a foundation of the real work. To be offered something that makes sense of your life, that is not judgemental and is also interesting and engaging early enough, provides a kind of hope that everyone needs. It makes it bearable then to see how one can recreate these patterns and the subsequent consequences and feelings without shame or blame. I think a lot of people do feel to blame at this stage, self-blame of course, but also being blamed by their therapists, who so often talk about their clients taking responsibility for all their life choices, without any awareness of why certain choices have been made. I consider this to be extremely harmful and can create more distress and confusion. It also indicates ignorance of how human beings function and the complexities of making choices when even the concept of choice as in childhood is completely inappropriate.

A good service shouldn't be a privilege for the few, but automatically a compassionate and effective service should be available for all: a service that I believe should be open to people to engage with and later if needed to re-engage with, especially for those who have had very traumatic experiences in early life.

As indicated earlier, I think the development of the work around recognising and working with the 'Neurotic Solutions' is very thorough and very useful and illuminating. When reading it, as well as following the theory and the 'case studies', I found myself thinking it would be really good to 'script' some sessions that would be imaginary but based on real life situations. Seeing how therapy sessions develop is often missing, in my experience, from training courses. What is helpful or not, to say to clients, how to move a session forward using these concepts etc. Comparing an Attachment-based session, using patterns and their connection to 'Neurotic Solutions', with CBT, to illustrate the differences, helping to define what works for people and what merely provides a 'sticking plaster'. I think a lot of GPs, counsellors, CPNs and certainly some psychiatrists and therapists simply don't know enough about how to promote long-lasting real change. I am aware that this is a big task and maybe a very cynical view of the current state of what is on offer to most people, but it is my conclusion.

The above of course leads one to think about appropriate and affordable training. I think the Attachment based training at the Bowlby Centre is about five years, very expensive and not easily available to people outside the capital. I would never want to imply that quality training can ever be done in a few weekend courses, but I do think there is some scope for all mental health practitioners to grasp the basic concepts over shorter courses, even if only a few of those go on to do proper psychotherapy training and work. I suppose what I am trying to say is that I think a good grounding in these concepts could alter the way that these clients are treated, assessed and ultimately helped to change their lives. We seem to have gone back to a state where the psychiatrist is at the top of the tree and only those who can afford private long-term psychotherapy stand any chance of getting a good enough deal. A lamentable state of affairs.

When I worked at the Edward Parry Mental Health Day Centre, run by Social Services in Kidderminster, we had a wide-ranging programme of group work. I was a facilitator in a number of women's groups where we used the idea of 'Life Patterns' as a starting point for the therapeutic work. Three workers contributed to a booklet explaining these ideas. We had mainly taken them from Joan Woodward's book 'Understanding Ourselves' and from her team supervision which she offered all of us for a period of time This came about through our desire as a team to work more therapeutically in a social work setting. At the time, most of the people that we worked with didn't receive any psychological therapy as they were considered not suitable. Many had been on huge doses of medication for years and years, but wanted something more than that.

Groups generally were very successful at the day centre. The most basic principle of sharing with others proved very uplifting and supportive, even to the most 'hopeless cases'. Women in particular value sharing their life stories with other women. They often formed friendships that were to last for years to come. We gradually introduced the ideas of John Bowlby, Jean Baker Miller, Alice Miller and Joan Woodward's eminently readable book. Some of these psychodynamic ideas are complex and formidable to the uninitiated, but Joan Woodward's work in particular makes it very accessible and understandable. I know this is something that she very much wanted to achieve with her book and I can testify to the fact that she did. Most of the women found the ideas interesting and, for some, life changing. There is an immediacy about thinking in terms of having a 'pattern' or several 'patterns' that can be identified, often without too much difficulty, and then to move on to what impact this has on your life now. Going through it stage by stage, giving a 'map' to follow and hazards on the way indicated. We spent a lot of time making the theory accessible and interesting, in the belief that a lot more people could benefit from this kind of work than usually get offered it. Of course we knew it wouldn't be all plain sailing, but the group support worked supremely well, particularly through quite a few patterns being similar to those of other people. Therapy can be a lonely business for a lot of people who have little support, so this approach worked well for most women. The group was on-going, so there weren't the time pressures workers have now. We did however have a programme and people were encouraged to work through it and then to 'live it a little' away from the group. We set up a support group alongside the therapy group, so there was somewhere for the women to move on to and they could return later if needed. This 'safety valve' was rarely abused and is something I believe is essential if people who have severe life-long problems are ever going to feel safe enough to manage their own lives. We actively encouraged the women to be in touch with each other outside of the group once the therapy period was over.'

To end my 'Response to this booklet', I want to add another human story that happened, unplanned and unexpected! I had a friend staying with me who has had long-term feelings of anxiety, especially about being alone. She wanted to enjoy the sun in the garden, which did not attract me, so I went to have a leisurely bath instead. She must have come in to see if I was downstairs again and seen a draft copy of this book on my desk. She took it out with her back into the garden. When I came down I saw through the window that she was engrossed in it. When she finished reading it, she came back in crying, saying so much of it 'struck home' and she could identify with so many parts of it. She said that she realised, more than ever before, how and why she had felt so anxious and depressed for so long. She has now decided to pursue some more help for herself with this knowledge and new understanding driving her to do so. I hope she will be able to find this.

Eleanor Wilkinson, adult nurse, wrote: 'I have found this book to be extremely interesting and informative. More importantly, I have found it very relevant and relatable to my own experiences of people with mental health problems. In particular, I find the concept of 'Neurotic Solutions' extremely fascinating. The idea that these negative, repetitive patterns of thinking could be caused by our early Attachment experiences is intriguing and, hopefully, could be very helpful in treating the many people who are suffering from these kinds of problems.'

Barbara Rickinson, retired counsellor, wrote: 'I was glad to be able to read and respond to this 'Short Account of Attachment Theory'. I was impressed with the author's clear description of the therapeutic relationship, which enables the recognition of painful patterns of thinking and behaving and an understanding of their source and perhaps the courage to change these old patterns for a more secure 'sense of self'. The author also notes from the therapeutic experience the difficulties encountered in making these changes even when they are desired.

I found Bowlby's Attachment Theory very relevant in my work with students at both Cambridge and Birmingham Universities. Bowlby made reference to the period of adolescence being an opportunity for psychological change, growth and development. I also found this to be true in relation to students' earlier Attachment histories and their ability to use the therapeutic relationship to develop a more secure 'sense of self'.'

A Therapy Client wrote: 'My parents waited a long time for children they weren't able to have. When I finally came along, at six weeks old, they were more than ready to give me all the love and affection I could possibly need. They made time for regular weekend camping trips and wonderful holidays by the sea. There were endless games of Lego and a bedtime story every night. My father would patiently instruct me on everything from how to climb a tree to how to catch the wave, at just the right moment, on a surf board. His own childhood had been in stark contrast to mine. His mother had died when he was three years old and his father hadn't returned from the Second World War. An aunt had taken him in, providing him with little warmth or affection. He was denied opportunities, such as an apprenticeship which was offered to him, in favour of bringing money into the home. He moved out, before meeting my mother, to live in nearby lodgings. When his own children came along he gave us, for many years, the love and affection denied him as a child. My sister and I felt loved, happy and secure. I thrived at school and for a long time couldn't have been happier.

Circumstances changed when I was around eleven years old. This was at a time when my father was frequently laid off work, due to 'strikes' at the factory where he worked. This placed my parents under enormous financial strain and it was only by going without themselves that they could maintain mortgage payments on their house. This pressure, together with my father's difficulty, due to his own childhood experiences, in coping with emotional stress, gave rise to feelings within him that became increasingly difficult for him to manage. A neighbouring family, living a few doors away, perhaps suspicious in those days of an adopted child with a great deal of energy, began to give accounts, to my parents, of the things I had supposedly said, or done – mostly in relation to their daughter who I played and went to school with. The accounts were unfounded but my father, maybe experiencing their criticism of me as a reflection upon him, was unable to provide any kind of a shield for me. Instead he would promise the neighbours that he would 'deal with' me. The punishment for a *crime* I hadn't committed would very likely be a 'damn good hiding'. This was mostly as it sounds and would leave me with red marks on my body, from the hard 'smacks' I'd receive. The firm grip he'd have, with his other hand, on some part of my arm, would be the only thing preventing me from falling, as each blow would knock me off my feet. At some stage my father must have deemed the punishment sufficient and it would come to an end, as would his rage. I don't know which felt worse – the sheer terror beforehand, as I anticipated the events about to happen, as I ran from him, pleading over and over for him not to 'hit me', or the feeling, in the immediate aftermath, of being utterly alone in the world.

My father's anger and rage was directed particularly towards me, as I increasingly disappointed him, and he seemed to need to push his own feelings of poor self-worth onto me. My sister, due to a medical condition, was a fragile child who certainly would not have been able to tolerate any physical duress. This also allowed her a level of protection from my father's expressions, or even his feelings, of anger, and they could maintain the close relationship now denied to me. My mother did, as she thought at the time to be the 'right thing to do', and stood behind the actions of her husband who, although finding it acceptable to bring such fear to his own child, would not have *dreamt* of hitting, or frightening, his wife. The control he had over me continued, in various ways, throughout my adolescence, when the smacking was replaced with verbal assaults, with him often telling me that I would be a 'failure in life' and 'never amount to anything'. These words, to this day, remain very clear in my mind, as I try to overcome the impact they had on me.

Whereas school had always been a place I'd enjoyed, another blow came at around twelve when I started High School. Placed in a 'top' class, I became separated from close friends and mostly from people I knew. Perhaps sensing vulnerability in me, I very soon, and for the first time, became a target of bullying from a small number of boys in my class. I experienced this bullying as another, familiar attack – this time on the happy secure feelings I had always had at school. The bullying escalated, becoming more severe, persistent and personal. I quickly became an outcast from the class, with no one wanting to risk their own position of relative 'safety' by speaking to me, in any other way than with distain. Similarly, no one dared speak up for me or reach out to anyone who may have been able to put a stop to it. I lived in utter dread of unsupervised time in school, either in the corridors and outside space or particularly when a teacher might need to leave the classroom for whatever reason and I would have no means of physically escaping the torment. My achievements diminished significantly and I became isolated and withdrawn for much of the time.

With little emotional support at home – which may have helped provide me with a different, more accurate, picture of myself – I could find no way of maintaining the belief I once had in myself and began to feel of no real worth. I believed the cruel words being repeated to me day after day, and came to feel their 'version' of me *had to be* the *correct one* and I became overwhelmed with feelings of shame and humiliation. I desperately sought ways, or 'solutions', which, I believed, would help protect me and also drew (what I now recognise to be false) conclusions about myself, in order to make some sort of sense of what was happening to me and to cope with the feelings I found so unbearable. These behaviours and thoughts, I have since come to understand, would become *my* 'Neurotic Solutions', that would persist long after ceasing to fulfil any useful purpose, bringing continuing suffering into my adult life.

In my late twenties I was fortunate to have been able to self-refer to a women's therapy centre. I gained an understanding of how, as a child, I would have needed to maintain my parents' much loved position. The only way I could do this was to turn the feelings of anger I felt towards *them*, inwardly onto *myself*, and felt guilt for 'causing' *them* to be so angry with *me*. Later, possibly in a similar way, it was the school bullies who, because of – as I saw it – their popularity with pupils and staff, *must* have been saying something of *worth* and that the 'fault' *again* lay with me. I began to see how these 'Neurotic Solutions' were now continuing to play a part in my reluctance to seek out new opportunities, friendships and relationships or just in fully taking part in life.

SOME NEUROTIC SOLUTIONS

1. I developed strong feelings in my teenage years of being 'ugly', as the bullies were repeatedly telling me – outlining daily in graphic detail – and this feeling progressed to a

feeling that I was 'offensive' to people, that I was somehow 'offending' *them* by the way I looked. I avoided mirrors and remember the precise moment I was unable to hold a teacher's gaze, through 'the shame of being me'. I have since found it difficult to maintain eye contact with people. My 'Neurotic Solution' perhaps being that by not looking at other people then perhaps *they* won't look at me and so see the flaws the bullies had made me so aware of.

2. I have found it necessary to 'prove', in the most exhausting of ways, that I am of 'value' – rather than accepting this as a 'given'. One example is how I continually seek to please people, believing that by doing so they would therefore like, and so value and respect, me. I have found difficulty in saying 'no' to people – particularly at work – and, on the occasions I have, I have experienced extreme anxiety. If I think that people think anything other than favourably of me then I feel compelled to go to great lengths to clarify my 'good' intentions and so be 'of worth' – in someone else's eyes.

3. I always try to ensure nothing I say or do can cause anyone to feel threatened, or provoke feelings of envy or jealousy. This 'solution', which, although sometimes keeping me out of the firing line at school, as an adult keeps me 'stuck' in a fearful position, avoiding success in many forms. It plays a part also in subtle forms of self-sabotaging behaviour, on occasions when I have managed to 'achieve' something good. Rather than keeping me 'safe', as originally intended, this 'meek' manner has created unhappiness, as I warily keep to the 'sidelines of life'.

4. I have found it almost impossible, through 'fear', to speak out, especially in a group situation of three or more. By

> maintaining silence I have sought to go unnoticed – always with the intention of reducing the risk of 'attack' or 'exposure' that could lead to further humiliation.

These Neurotic Solutions, as I understand them and have attempted to describe, have brought me continuing suffering and had a lasting impact on my life. I have found it difficult to establish and maintain friendships and relationships, finding it difficult to relax and be around other people, and I have spent much time without the regular company of others. I have not particularly progressed in a career, finding it difficult to talk about my work with colleagues. However, in my day-to-day work as a teacher, I have **always** made sure I maintain a safe environment, where no one feels intimidated or uncomfortable and that learning can take place for everyone. *In this I know I have been successful!*

I would love to be able to report that the awareness of, and understanding as to why I acquired, these Neurotic Solutions has enabled me to finally be rid of them; and so bring about change and relief in me. Instead, as the author writes about in this book, I find I am persisting in holding onto these solutions for 'dear life'. The real 'work' for me is taking place a lot more recently, as I try to examine more fully my reluctance in letting go of these Neurotic Solutions and why I cling onto the 'safety' of the 'Z' position, even though it brings continuing suffering for me. If I could dare move towards an 'A' position – to have good feelings about myself again, as I'd experienced in early childhood – then surely I would have a more fulfilling life? I think a big part of my fear, and so reluctance to do this, is in anticipating that the move from the 'Z' to the 'A' position would bring with it the potential for someone to again *take* these good feelings from me, as had happened not once, but twice, in my early life. The pain, and feelings of 'injustice', when *losing the original 'A' position* – particularly the feelings of security and self-worth that my father had helped create in me – had been overwhelming at the time. To now experience a new 'A' position, and to risk a 'backlash' of having it *taken* from me again, feels very scary. And so part of my work is in the battle to *hold onto* the belief that now *only I* can *give* those feelings away – that they cannot be *taken* from me again and that I *do not* have to *'pay a price'* for living in the 'A' position.

I hope this has given some insight into my own struggle; I have been able to take from the book the need to keep check of the 'old' thoughts and feelings as they arise. In striving to be free of the old patterns of thinking and behaving, the first step is *'to recognise* 'Z' thinking'. The second step is *'to reject* 'Z' thinking' and the third step is *'to act'*. It is the process of *'acting'* that now has most significance for me. In the author's words, it is:

"Important TO ACT in order to 'not allow the old 'Z' pattern to continue to dominate' and 'if making a real change can be seen as *not* something that has all to be done *today*', as this can then so readily be seen as 'far too big a mountain to climb'. If change can be seen instead as something to recognise, reject and then to act differently towards, just at moments, some notion of how it might really happen begins to emerge that feels less terrifying, or impossible. Above all, the person has experienced not having to obey the 'Z' voice has not led to anything dreadful happening. Even if only for a few moments, they have had a sense of feeling 'different', calmer and more in charge of themselves and being how they deep down want to be, feeling secure in themselves."'

<u>Shirley Price, retired admin. assistant in a university Finance department</u>, wrote: 'For a long time 'people watching' has been a great interest of mine. When I read this book, I felt that I knew all the people discussed in it! It made me understand a lot more about life and the struggles some people have with it.

I think we all need to be valued, but we all need to be SHOWN that we are! I think valuing ourselves is of utmost importance to me, which the author obviously understands. I found this book interesting and enlightening.'

ACKNOWLEDGMENTS

My primary thanks goes to my son, David Woodward, for rescuing me with utmost patience at the many 'crisis moments' I had with my computer. Without his help, this book would never have been completed.

My thanks also go to Trevor Brown, Alice Solomons and the FAB team for seeing this book not only worth publishing, but as the start of a series of short books.

I owe my warmest thanks to all the contributors to section five for their amazing readiness to share their personal responses to the book.

Joan Woodward